AF377894

HEART CONNECTION

*The **POWER** to **CREATE**
the Life you want!*

HEART CONNECTION

The *POWER* to *CREATE* the Life you want!

Marie-Josée Laquerre

ISBN: 978-2-37011-763-2
Éditions Hélène Jacob – 13 Impasse Victor Gesta – 31200 Toulouse – France
US$ 20,45
Printed by Amazon KDP
April 2025

Cover design: Marie-Josée Laquerre
Cover layout: Kim Trudel
Translation: Traductions LFV
Typographical revision: Hélène Jacob
Graphic design of the summary tables: Annie-Kim Verdon
Photographer: Michel Lafortune (pictures of the author)

To the people I love so much, your presence fills me with **"Happiness."** *Yes! Your ever-loving presence has greatly contributed to this book, not to mention your compassionate and generous help during the most difficult times or when I doubted myself during the writing process.*

I thank you with all my **"Heart"** *for being a part of my Life! Thank you to the guidance,* **"Source of life,"** *to the* **"mentors"** *and to the* **"great wise ones"** *that have been my teachers throughout my life and gave me the inspiration to create the wellness techniques in this book.*

These techniques have always been necessary and helped me overcome my fears, free myself from some blockages and recover my life balance during unsettling times.

Alternating these techniques regularly has had a positive impact on my emotional, physical, mental and spiritual health.

A positive outcome that helps me live, as much as possible, in the joy of the **"Heart Connection."** *These helpful tools give me a significant and happy advantage in my daily life in order to create my little "SME" of happiness! (My little daily joys.)*

MERCI la Vie!

"Choosing your Heart is choosing happiness!"

Marie-Josée Laquerre

Preface

A Word from the Author

*D*ear readers,

Writing this book has been a true pleasure for me, especially since I had not even planned to write a book in my lifetime. I had a lot of ambitions, but not this one!

*It was when I was going through the biggest "***Life Transition***" of my life that this project began. A year and a half without any rest or time to return to my roots, going from one ordeal to the other without catching a break. I did not have time to recover from one situation that another one would come up, as difficult as the last one, without any warning!*

The teachings I have received while writing this book helped me go through what seemed to be the biggest crisis of my life. The regular use of these amazing tools allowed me to free myself from a lot of emotions, from all my "Overflows" and to put my mind to rest. The overflow of anxiety, anguish, stress and distress that I had to overcome to get back to a calm and peaceful state regardless of the circumstances (not to say the Tsunamis!) coming through my life.

*It is by practicing the "**Transition to nothingness**" technique that I could develop the Faith I needed to go through such an unsettling process. A process that sometimes makes us feel a great emptiness inside, that makes us go through many losses, disappearances and abandonment, that forces us to see all of our personal resources weaken and lose all of our bearings, that makes us cope with the loneliness and face different stages of grief and go through the intensity of a "**Life Transition**."*

As you can see, it's not that fun! But at the end of the day, I could feel that Life would always have my back, no matter what. After having many major difficulties during this period, I can now say confidently that Life has been good to me. Nonetheless, I have had many confirmations and proofs of its support, through small miracles of Life or by the presence of faithful and sincere people, even during the worst times.

♥ Short Story of This "Life Transition" ♥

It all started when I sold my Balneotherapy and Massage Therapy Spa I had owned for 18 years. After selling it, it proved to be quite difficult to start a new career. I did not have the expected result and success despite the fact that I had invested a lot of time and a lot of money.

At the same time, my husband also went through a major career change after working for 25 years at the same organization. In spite of us, this was imposed upon him too. It really shook up our relationship as both of our financial situations became unstable. We were scared and came very close to losing all of our assets and real estate that we had worked for over the last 20 years, resulting in many sleepless nights experiencing all kinds of anxieties and stress.

During this period, I also had several losses, nine in total: the passing of three aunts and uncles and three close family friends, I assisted in my father's end-of-life care, his passing followed by a very complicated and hard-to-deal-with succession for ten months, and the loss of my 103-year-old grandmother with whom I had a deep relationship. Also, we lost our pet. Our beautiful little cat Maya, whom I considered part of our family as she was such a sweet and tender being and showered us with unconditional love. We get so attached to our little pets!

All of these draining events had the effect of an enormous life tornado. A **"Forced Transition to nothingness"** *was necessary to go through a* **"Life Transition"** *and better our future. I do not talk about all my hardships to complain, even if during this transition I often felt like I was taken hostage by Life. I sometimes saw myself as a victim who was unable to get through it. I share all these personal and vulnerable experiences of my life in order to show that Life is, without a doubt, fragile for all of us even when we think we are protected from all of these hardships. Life can change in the blink of an eye.*

Everyone has problems and hardships in their daily life. We all have, at some point, to go through an important **"Life Transition"** *and make changes for our well-being. In these trying times, Life shows us that everything can quickly change and often when we least expect it. This is what happened to me after years of great abundance, joy and happiness. There is always a gift at the end, but when you are going through something difficult, it is harder to see!*

Nonetheless, I have always had the feeling that I did my best, I have been very generous in my life and gave a lot through my career, to my family, my friends and even to charities with great generosity. I did it with the intention of "giving back" the abundance, the prosperity and the time that I had in order to help others in my own way. I have always shared happily. All things considered, you can understand why I asked myself many times why I was going through these great ordeals. You will find the answer as you read this book… Suspense!

One thing is certain, I had to deal with many losses and go through each stage of grief. I had to take a step back in order to comfort, heal and gradually soothe my sadness. I had to overcome the feeling of loss that I had from losing all these people I loved very much. I had to take a step back from all these imponderable events of Life and let go of the way I had lived before… Phew! Easy! LOL!

All of this has forced me to make sacrifices and compromises of all sorts. In short, a lot of letting go, but the result is surprising! I would even say beneficial for what it brought me in the end.

This book is meant for everyone who is going through important changes in their lives. Whether it be a career change, a new direction, moving to a new city or country, a family or marital adjustment, health problems, financial difficulties, an unexpected world event or an "Overflow" from daily life, it does not matter…

*"**The Heart Connection**" is a useful and practical tool to help you recenter yourself every day and free yourself from everything that is going wrong in your life. It can also help if something is holding you back from following your life journey and reaching your objectives. The exercises that you will discover (the ones I did during this transition and still do) are really useful to bring you back in the right mindset, in a place of joy, love, health and abundance, in the truth of your deepest ambition and in the feeling of trust that I feel about Life.*

*By freeing myself from all of my "overflows," I feel much more capable to peacefully go through life with a great inner conviction that "**The Heart Connection**" really creates "**Miracles in Life**" for myself and for others!*

Give it a go, the results are surprising, it heals the heart, resolves problematic situations and transforms them into happy ones! I have had so many little miracles of Life happen to me during this transformation that I could write an entire book about them.

I wish you all the same! With all my Heart's Love!
Happy reading!

Marie-Josée Laguerre

Chapter 1

The "Transition to Nothingness" Technique

When life asks you to do a "transition to nothingness," it means that there is an "overflow" that needs to be released. Throughout this book, I will often talk about the notion of "overflow" because it is the result of emotional blockages and a great deal of suffering that happens in our lives which negatively impacts our achievements.

One day, despite all my efforts, I realized that nothing came to me. I had the sensation that my life was suddenly turned upside down. My relentless efforts to be fulfilled and successful, as I was used to, were in vain. Nothing that I did seem to work, as if everything I had learned, practiced and experienced was useless. I was caught off guard because for the past year I had listened very closely to what Life was telling me to do at any given moment. I was in tune with my intuition and my inner voice. A few months earlier, I had made a big change in my life: I sold the business I had managed for 18 years in order to teach and share the knowledge I had acquired throughout the years in the health and wellness industry. My intuition spoke strongly and told me to share all of my "Health Favorites."

This change required and demanded an enormous amount of courage from me because it took me out of my "comfort zone" and threw me into the unknown, without any of the consistency or financial stability that I had been used to for so long.

My inner voice was talking to me louder and louder and I finally had no choice but to listen to it. For too long, the same sensations and images had been surfacing in my mind incessantly. It is said that when you feel the same inspiration and when you picture yourself doing the same thing three times, it is Life guiding you to do it and showing you the right path to take. These thoughts, intuitions and images manifested themselves in my mind for three years before I took the big leap…

It was time to face my fears! No, but really, when you need to receive a message, Life makes sure you get it by any means possible! You always think about it, you have intuitions about the future, you dream about it, you talk about it, people talk to you about it, and yet, you do nothing!

And the cycle starts over and over! NO, do something, it's easy!

You just have to choose to "choose to do something" … so simple!

During those three years, I slowly started the transition toward my new objectives and I put some guidance into action while continuing to manage my business. But life is no fool! Ha! You think you can do it all, that you can hold on to your safety and have total faith in Life!

"Well, I got some news for you, my friend! You still have to take a big leap… one day or another… and finally listen to what your Heart is telling you!"

I finally sold my business to throw myself into the "emptiness" of my future. Although I was slowly preparing my "future self" during these past years, the fact remained that someday I would have to face this "transition to nothingness" which, let's face it, disrupts all the aspects of our existence.

My old ways were no longer working. All of a sudden, I had no guideline to successfully achieve what I wanted to do. Yet, in my life, everything I had done had been successful from the beginning, but now… I was suddenly facing one disappointment after the other in every aspect of my life. My life was falling apart at the very moment I was expecting renewal, a new beginning and a rebirth after I had found the courage to fully listen to Life's messages. I tried all my old ways of "doing" until I realized that there was nothing left to "do." I was like a lost sheep in the center of my own universe, living moments of anxiety and worry that made me suffer for several months.

Even my friends the deer did not recognize me! LOL!

I kept on practicing all of my Tao/Yoga/Meditation and Pranayama (Breathing Techniques) in order to purify myself from my old life and from the past. I was momentarily relieved while practicing the teachings I had received from the masters, but as soon as I got back in action, I lost all divine guidelines.

All my life, I was someone who took action and loved to accomplish things, but now I was living the biggest "forced transition to nothingness" of my life. I felt like I was losing everything, even my own identity.

What a strange sensation! In fact, I was experiencing my own death while I was still alive. Pretty unsettling if you ask me!

I felt all the emotions: worry, anxiety, sorrow, disappointment, anger, sadness, displeasure, injustice and fear. YES!

It was a little unfair to go through all of that after making such great efforts to get there and to finally find nothing. So, why had Life guided me there?

I was angry at Life and asked myself what it wanted from me. I had the feeling that I was meeting all of its demands, but without any obvious or beneficial result. At one point, I did not want to live anymore… What was the point? I needed to find a solution to what I was going through… being more and more lost… but my friends the deer did not come to save me!

I was surprised to feel this way, I had always been such a happy person, a source of joy and a ray of sunshine to those around me. These moments, when they come, shock those around us – our significant others, our family, our friends. When they come, those major changes are noticeable in our language, in our daily habits and in the way we live. During this transition, we can even be surprised by this new person, this new "Me" that shows itself in the open, like a totally different person than the one we were before!

One day, as I was sitting on my favorite rock by the water, I was in total contemplation of nature's beauty when this beautiful eagle came to glide over my head. It glided into the air in big circles, effortlessly, letting the wind and Life carry it without any worry. What a great lesson it gave me that day! As if it was carrying a special message just for me, a message that really resonated within me! Yes, that day, it came to me, and in that moment, I realized that I had had enough. Enough of making every effort to succeed, to be my best self, to organize my whole life like a "Wonder Woman," always doing more and more… to be able to "do" it all. I just wanted to let Life carry me like the wind carried the eagle, to let go and follow the flow of this generous, abundant and prosperous Life. At the same time, I realized I was living a great "transition to nothingness"… the total emptiness of not wanting anything anymore. I then took three months to reach nothingness, to live my transition, and to do what was necessary for my well-being.

During that period, Life had strangely occupied all of my time with my father's multiple and urgent health problems; we almost lost him on three occasions. Strangely, I was seeing the imminent death of my father and, at the same time, I was experiencing my own death, even though my body was in perfect physical condition. The death I was experiencing was this "transition to nothingness." The feeling of having nothing inside is a strong and unsettling feeling for anyone who is used to manage their own life, to take the reins willingly and have a real sensation of control!

Life was asking me to surrender, to let go, and the more I did, the more this feeling of "nothing" grew… Until the day I decided to focus on it. If Life wanted to take me into the "nothingness" then why not go for it? Why not dive in? After all, I had learned to "dive" when I was young! (lol!) But I quickly realized that it was not the same type of diving!

I knew what diving into the unknown felt like, I had done it more than once in my life. Like the time I opened up a Spa in Guadeloupe, and other times when I changed careers, moved to a new city, etc.

Diving into the unknown was something I knew! It should have been easy, but it was NOT! Even if I had experienced emptiness and the unknown at other times in my life, this time, it was not pleasant and joyful for my mental health. It also brought back many fears to the surface … fears I had to learn to manage.

♥ 1 | Why Try to Reach This "Nothingness"? ♥

We try to reach this "nothingness" because there is an "overflow" of too many things at once. That is why there is a "forced" transition to nothingness.

It is like a glass of water that is filled to the brim, if you add more, it will overflow.

That is exactly what I was going through, everything was overflowing, there was too much, way too much! I then started the process of releasing the "overflows" of my life. Release the "overflow" of responsibilities, the "overflow" of work, the "overflow" of organizing the life of the "Super Woman" that took care of everything: managing my business 24/7 for 18 years, managing the house and the estate, the renovations, budgeting, family meetings, outings, vacations, friends, leisure activities, all of that while being a great wife, friend, family member and trying to take care of myself! Wow!!! … The "Super Woman!" Do you recognize her?

"Super Woman or Super Man?"

OOF! A big relaxing sigh to let it all out, but Life goes on faster and faster. So, how do I get through it all with my busy schedule?

Out of breath, I started to practice the "transition to nothingness" technique. A technique to relax every day and access my inner nothingness, putting myself in sync with it, be a part of it and abandon myself completely to it.

It is only by liberating this "overflow" and by reaching this nothingness that we can empty our glass of water and fill it again … unless we drink it!

The Universe is made that way and Life knows exactly what it is doing even if we sometimes forget! In fact, we need to stop "Doing" in order to start "Being." Not an easy thing to do when you are in the whirlwind of daily life and need to follow society's requirements of productivity, effectivity and performance. Yes! Society values our success through excessive and efficient work. Have you ever had a boss that congratulated you for doing less work? … The answer is probably NO! :))

If we learn to "Be" and we take the time to just "Be," Life will take care of "Doing" for us. How interesting!

YES! Life will "Do" for you because it will bring you what you need at the right time, especially if you take time to adapt to your personal rhythm, to Life's rhythm and to the Breath of the Universe. When we listen to our "Self," we save a lot of time that would be wasted in the whirlwind of Life.

You might think that it is a lot to learn, and you would be right. It is a whole different programing (or deprogramming) than the one we currently have in our brain. I managed my business for 18 years by following my intuitions to make decisions for the team of therapists, the clients, the administration management, the marketing, the budgeting, etc.

With all the new and fast vibrations of the Universe that activated at the end of 2012, we are in a new era that now asks us to go from "Doing" to "Being." The things that happened before by "Doing" now have to come to us by the feeling of "Being" first and foremost, otherwise nothing can happen exactly like we want it to happen in our mind.

Humans must come back to their "Inner Selves" so that their "Outer selves" can be the reflection of their real convictions and their deepest ambitions. Doing for the sake of doing does not cut it anymore, Life asks us to learn how to simply "Be." To achieve this, there is the "transition to nothingness." A "transition to nothingness" to purify the ancient ways of "Doing" in order to learn how to "Be." Pretty complicated!

♥ 2 | The "Transition to Nothingness" Technique ♥

<u>Here is an example of the "Transition to nothingness" Technique:</u>
1) Relax through meditation, sit comfortably or lie in bed (if you are able to stay awake).

2) Take three long and deep breaths. When you exhale, "release" as much as possible. Exhale three times completely until you are out of breath, as if your abdomen was holding your breath from the inside.

3) Connect yourself to the great nothingness of the Universal Source. Imagine a great and clear hole in the Sky, visualize a place where there is a "big swirling spiral in the Universe" in which you can release all of your "overflows" with each exhale. With its centrifugal force, this majestic spiral takes in everything and transforms it into a love energy that is beneficial for all.

Centrifugal Force of the "Great Spiral of the Universe"

4) Go through each of your "overflows" of life and release them, using your hands, in the "great nothingness" hole. Let go of every "overflow" in the "spiraling drain" and watch them disappear completely.

"Great Nothingness" Hole of the Spiraling Drain

Let go of the "overflows" of the workday, the "overflows" of tiredness, the "overflows" of disappointment, of sadness and of sorrow. Let go of the responsibilities of work, family or love.

Free yourself from the "overflows" of financial worry, the "overflows" of anxiety, of anger, of unspoken things or of any other "overflows" that come to mind. Let go and free yourself completely with every exhale. No need to think of a precise situation that you went through or any emotional distress in your life. Just let go of the "overflow," the "Self" that feels they have too much on their plate, their body, their soul, their heart and their mind.

5) At the end of each meditation, put your hands on your Heart with your right hand over the left. Breathe three times deeply while feeling the power of the "inner emptiness" that you just activated.

6) Open your arms wide to embrace Life's energy, bring that energy toward you and close your hands on your Heart. Do it three times to open and embrace the benefits of Life and concentrate them on your Heart. How do you feel? Without knowing it, you just experienced the **"Heart Connection!"** By opening up, you can be thankful for all this love that you carry, and thank Life for always taking care of you. It is always there for us, even if we do not always realize it.

7) As you do this exercise, let go of all the "overflows" of tension in the body: the tense muscles, the knots, the blockages. Target the part in your body where there is more "overflows," and as you exhale, release it. If there is a feeling that emerges from this tension, let it go at the same time. No need to rethink a situation that is in the past or to see it in your mind, just let go of the feeling associated with it. No need to go over an emotional situation or recreate it in your body and your mind. When you exhale, create only nothingness from that situation.

Exhale three times until you feel the emptiness from your lungs to your lower abdomen. Empty, unload and evacuate everything, all the way to your nerve endings. Let go of the "overflow" of your muscles, of your blood flow, of the tensions in the head, and connect yourself to the Universal Source mentioned earlier.

In the Universal process, everything is similar and identical for all Life. Everything that lives on Earth, whether it be plants, animals or humans, everywhere there is Life, for all organisms, there is a need to consume food and evacuate the waste. The "great nothingness" process is everywhere, even nature cleanses itself constantly. The leaves fall from the trees in autumn to come back the next spring.

8) If you have severe pain, burning or inflammation in your body, release the "overflow" where there is pain and breathe out deeply until you no longer feel pain or until you feel a release, a lightness. Release the weight of the "overflows" from the responsibilities of life, work, family, friends, sorrow and sadness. Release the "overflow" of emotions such as anger, bitterness, hatred and guilt. Empty your glass of water or your bucket of water if there is a lot! Sometimes we accumulate a lot more than we think… So, clear absolutely everything out!

Always visualize that you are releasing everything into the "clear hole" of the "**giant spiral of the Universe**" in which everything flows. It is the power of the Universal Source that clears everything out for you. Feel the centrifugal movement take everything that you no longer need and free yourself from it.

9) And then, as you exhale, fill your mind with the power of the Universal Source. Do the same thing for your whole body three more times. Let the abundance of the Universal Mother carry you, fill you with her graces, her blessings, and open your Heart to receive. And now, feel, feel, feel … this inner wellness.

The more you practice this "transition to nothingness" technique, the more you allow Life to "fill" you with all its blessings. When you do this exercise every day, you release what has no longer a reason to

"Be" and start to feel the benefits and blessings of Life, since **Life and the Universe do not tolerate emptiness.** In order to let Life fill us up with blessings, gratitude, joys and happiness we need to release those "overflows" that prevent us from receiving the new things that Life has to offer!

Doing this exercise every day allows us to experience a rebirth, to open up to new things and to experience Life's surprises. Life takes care of finding solutions to our problems and guides us properly toward better actions. After only five days of practicing the "transition to nothingness" liberation technique, I have personally experienced four small miracles of Life. As if some difficult situations had resolved themselves.

Merci la Vie ! ... Gratitude

The more we practice the "transition to nothingness" technique, the more we will wake up excited to discover everything Life has in store for us regarding our wellness and our happiness! Pay attention to all the surprises that Life will bring you and write them down, because there will be more of them, like sudden "Miracles."

Life will become an endless blessing! It is our turn to enjoy it, because the more we listen to the "Self" and to what we deeply aspire to, the more Life allows us to meet our true needs.

The entire Universe conspires for our "Happiness" and puts everything into place to ensure that we are perfectly happy… It's the Law of Life!

The Heart of the Universe

Chapter 2

How Can We Release the "Overflow"?

How should we empty the glass or the bucket of water? By using the "transition to nothingness" technique seen in the previous chapter. But why should we do it?

Since water transforms everything and our body is made of 70% of it, reaching nothingness by using the "transition to nothingness" technique can free us a bit more, it is a cleansing and purifying process that occurs naturally in the body. Water is tied to our emotions and our emotional body, all the disturbing emotions that end up creating the veil from our life's reality stem from it.

Emotions like anger, sadness, disappointment, anxiety, concern, doubt, and fear can drag us away from where we want to be. The veil of the emotional body becomes too dense and our "Self" no longer has its rightful place because the cloud of emotions is too heavy.

Drinking a big glass of water is also recommended when we go through strong emotions since it is soothing and it tempers the current emotion while also purifying the emotional body. Try it out! You will see how helpful it is and how it allows us to see an ambiguous and sometimes dramatic situation with more clarity.

The more emphasis we put on an emotion, the more we allow it to grow within us. The more we feed the anger, the more violent it becomes. The more we feed the fear, the harder it becomes to overcome it which prevents us from living in our Heart. By recreating a concern within our thoughts or by focusing on our anxiety, we relive these emotions in our life even more. These emotions take up more and more space, and it becomes a never-ending vicious cycle.

When we keep talking about our emotions, our tragedies, our anger and our disappointments, we feed our emotional body and give it more importance than it deserves instead of focusing on our real identity: the "Self." We recreate the same emotions to try to free ourselves from them! We have to stop giving them so much importance, because it only makes them grow … let's focus on our true desires, our projects and our life goals.

Careful, it's not about ignoring an emotion, running from it or pushing it aside, because the pot will eventually boil over! You need to be aware of what you feel, to assess the state of the wound to heal and transform it with the "transition to nothingness" technique.

Love that comes from the Universal Source gives us everything, and the more we realize it, the more this process can heal us and free us from karmas and negative attitudes, transforming them into wellness, health, joy and happiness. By practicing the "transition to nothingness" technique, the "overflow" of emotions is released without having to work on ourselves, to mentally dissect the uneasy feelings or to analyze the meaning behind it. The answers come naturally and often with great clarity.

Resorting to different methods to better understand our mental state, either through personal development, NLP, psychology or some form of therapy is all beneficial to our emotional and mental state, improves our understanding of the event and helps us through our journey of personal growth if we need it. However, it is not always necessary to go through all of that for every fleeting emotion or every "overflow." Those methods often make us relive our emotions, our sadness, our anger, our bitterness or our anxiety, and expands this emotional zone … even if it makes us feel better for a moment.

Some methods go as far as suggesting that we give a name to our different emotions. This unfortunately keeps them alive and allows them to get bigger and stronger as it gives them importance, energy and attention. As we know, the more energy we put on something, the more likely it is to happen again, and again, and again! The first step is to analyze our state of "SELF" by using the methods listed above. Once it is done, the second step is to give in to the "transition to nothingness" technique, because the Universal Source takes care of the rest for us. No need to rack our brains to understand! Understanding is not always necessary! What an amazing gift from Life! MERCI LA VIE !

Since humans have a mental body, we like to understand everything. In most cases, analyzing our situation is part of the process.

However, the *"**Grand Masters**" are there to show us that the "transition to nothingness" can be done without having to analyze everything from the beginning. They all work with the strength of the Universal Source of nothingness. All the teachings from the *"**Masters**" favor the "emptiness" of the mental plane and the emotional body. They teach us Meditation, Yoga, Tao, "Pranayama" breathing techniques, the art of silence for ten days or two weeks, etc. These are all techniques that ease the liberation process of the "overflows" and they are compatible with the "transition to nothingness" purification. (For more information on these different Liberation Techniques, see Chapter XI)

♥ 1 | "Transition to Nothingness" and Letting Go ♥

The "transition to nothingness" fills us with energy, raises our Prana level (vital energy source) and fills our mind with new ideas, thoughts, intuitions and inspirations. It also connects us with the Divine sacred energy. It is the best way to let go, to give in and to let our fate in Life grow! Because, as we know, when we let go, everything falls into place like magic!

Careful, doing the "transition to nothingness" and letting go does not mean to do nothing, to abolish action or to stop generously investing in ourselves. It does not mean to stop getting up in the morning to work or to wait around and expect everything to happen like magic!

As the saying goes: "Without hard work, nothing grows but weeds."

We need to act and go toward our "Life Mission" that we feel belongs to our "Self." It means that we let go of what we no longer want in our life, that we release our "overflow" daily and that we free the veil of our mental and emotional body. Above all, we have to consciously realize that the Universal Source guides all our actions in life, every day, at all times. We need to have an unshakeable faith in ourselves and in Life!

Then, and only then, can we say "MERCI LA VIE!"

♥ 2 | Thriving Materially While Having a Spiritual Awakening ♥

We have to fulfill our mission with an unshakeable fate. Every human on Earth has the same main incarnation mission: **"Thriving**

materially while having a spiritual awakening." One cannot go without the other.

Uniting the Earth and the Sky, reaching a balance with the material aspects through the spiritual dimension. It can be done with any career or life mission … as long as it is done in the respect of the profound convictions and aspirations of our "Self." The balance between the two is unique for everybody, therefore you have to choose how to unite those two aspects of life with as much balance as possible.

This is what we are meant to experience and to learn. No matter the path we will choose or take, the goal is the same for everyone: the balance of these two dimensions, "the material and the spiritual."

Ha! Many of you must have had a totally different conception of Heaven on Earth, to eat Philadelphia Cream Cheese on a cloud as seen on television or to relax, more often than not, in a hammock by the sea while reading a good book and drinking a mojito! How fun would that be? Sorry to disappoint! Life has something else planned for us, even if taking a break under the sun is greatly appreciated and necessary from time to time to allow us to recharge our batteries!

We are on Earth to "materially thrive" and "awaken spiritually" through our parents, our families, our environments, our community, our culture, our city, our country and all the choices that we have made before our birth in order to grow and live our human and terrestrial adventure. Thanks to our free will, it is up to us to choose what suits us best to be happy! Easy to say, but not so easy to do.

When Jesus said: "Many are called, but few are chosen," he was certainly not talking about eating Philadelphia Cream Cheese on a cloud! He was actually talking about having the courage to realize ourselves beyond our fears, blockages and obstacles of all kinds that are preventing us from following our ultimate goal: "to Be Happy!" Therefore, the "chosen ones" are those who have the strength, the courage and the will to truly "Be Happy" … and to act accordingly … not those who only want to eat cheese! Ha ha!

Here is a Meditation Technique in three quick, simple and efficient steps designed to ease our way onto the path of our destiny and to reach our main goal: "Be Happy!"

♥ 3 | Meditation Technique ♥

How to release the "overflows" … in three quick, simple and efficient steps.

First step
Relax. Inhale and exhale deeply three times.

Second step
With each exhales, start to release all your "overflows" … visualize that you are releasing all your "overflows" in the "**clear hole**" of the giant "**Spiral of the Universe**" as seen in the "Transition to nothingness" technique in Chapter I.

▶ Release all your "overflows" of guilt.

▶ Release your "overflows" of sensibility, vulnerability, fragility and innocence that make you experience many inconveniences.

▶ Release the "overflows" of anger and frustrations related to your work, your daily life, your family or your married life.

▶ Release the "overflows" of "I have to's" and the never-ending "to-do" lists.

▶ Release the "overflows" of the efforts you "have" to do in order to succeed, to be productive or to reach your goals and objectives.

▶ Release the "overflows" of perseverance, determination, endurance or chores.

▶ Release the "overflows" of negative and self-destructive thoughts or depressed states.

▶ Release the "overflows" of internal conversations and mental ruminations.

▶ Release the "overflows" of your discouragements caused by societal pressure.

▶ Release the "overflows" of blockages and ego resistance as well as moral, mental, emotional and physical sufferings.

Then, take three to five deep breaths and repeat the process until you feel that you have released everything there is to release, as shown previously in the "Transition to nothingness" technique.

<u>Third step</u>

Once it is done, you can begin the filling process. For each breath, make sure you fill both your mind and your entire body with peace, calmness, love, balance, joy, serenity, fullness, goodness, courage, strength, quiet power, health, healing, etc. You can also choose anything you need to "fill" yourself with. It differs from person to person and is based on what you need at a given moment.

Breathe in only positive things. Picture things you love to "Be" and pay attention to the way it makes you feel in your body. Fill yourself with love, peace, justice, truth, wisdom, knowledge, compassion, altruism, creativity, originality, pleasure, laughter, etc. It's up to you!

Happy relaxation, happy meditation!

Chapter 3

The "Heart Connection"

The "**Heart Connection**" cannot be achieved if there are blockages, resistance or "overflows" in our relationships or in our life since every resistance or blockage also bring suffering, no matter what they are.

Resisting = Suffering is a rule to remember. Realizing it allows us to let go faster. If we experience an emotional resistance caused by disappointment, anger or sadness, it will prevent us from seeing the reality of the situation because it builds a wall around us. This wall brings a lot of suffering and incomprehension. The reality is often much different. We simply need to look at it differently than with our own perception and limitations.

For example, it can be important for someone to be thanked after giving something. For them, acknowledgement and politeness are crucial in their way of doing things, and they will often be disappointed by someone else's approach if it is not expressed in the same way.

In this example, the "**Resistance**" is the disappointment of not receiving the "Thank you" they expected. It will create tension between the two people, which can lead to a major disagreement, preventing the "Heart Connection."

Opening our mind and our conscience to see that our way to be thankful and grateful can differ from someone else can release this heart-to-heart resistance. This person could do it differently, either by using gestures instead of words, or by doing something thoughtful for the other person. It could surprise us since it is done in ways we did not expect.

Seeing things differently opens the "Heart Connection"
with everyone and every situation in Life.

When we say "I love you" or "you are pretty" to someone, the gift is initially for us since saying it with the Heart brings joy, and we also get to see someone receive our compliments joyfully. On the other hand, if the other person never compliments us, they can express their love by making us laugh, by taking care of us with various thoughtful gestures or by sharing their abundance in different ways. For example, they could pay for us during an outing, take us out to the restaurant, bring us a gift, etc. The list can be long. When we see that the other person opens their Heart for us instead of having expectations and experiencing resistance toward them, the "Heart Connection" operates like magic and love can flow freely.

The disruption with the "Heart Connection" happens because of the differences between what we expect to receive and what we give to others. Life has a lot of ways to fulfill us, we just need to open our eyes to see further and discover new avenues than the ones we already know.

The Heart is at the center of our life, the Heart is at the center of our body. The Heart is the fourth energy vortex ("Chakra") of our body. It is the link between the Earth and the Sky, between the material and the spiritual.

We have to focus with the infinite power of the Heart in order to reach a balance between the material and the spiritual planes. As soon as there is destabilization or "suffering," it is a sign from Life that we need to come back to the Heart.

For example, if we feel distressed, depressed, anxious or worried, it is a message from Life that "clearly" says to come back to the "Heart" and to the "Heart Connection" instead of spiraling into mental assumptions that might never come true.

Life asks us to always listen to our "Heart" for what we truly want, for what we want to experience, and to take action to make it happen.

If we take action to make our Heart's desires come true, Life will give us the possibilities to fulfill them.

Consequently, our vital energy is increased since we are not going against what we truly feel. Life then starts to give us many gifts… Merci la Vie ! We just need to listen to it!

The "***Grand Masters**" teach us that Life flows on its own and that, apparently, we do not have to put up a big fight to reach our goals. If we fight, it might be a sign that we are not in synergy or aligned with the "Heart Connection." Remember those moments when you are doing something you truly love and how Life is suddenly easy, joyful and happy… In those moments, there is no need to fight and we do not feel as if we have to make any type of effort. We can take action without losing energy. It flows naturally and Life gives us what we aspire to, simply because we do what we love with our Heart. That is when we feel as if we were living on a cloud … even though we are on Earth!

♥ 1 | Exercise: The List of "LOVE TO BE'S!" ♥

Making the list of what we love to "BE" activates the Law of Attraction and creates the movement that allows us to reach our goals. Even if our reality does not exactly correspond to what we love, making the list of what we **"LOVE TO BE"** and repeating it regularly can make what we desire in our life happen more quickly.

Reading your list or saying it out loud every morning and every evening allows you to realize and manifest your "LOVE TO BE'S" a lot faster!

I personally say my list out loud when I wake up, I say it again when I get ready for the day, when I pamper myself and even when I do the dishes or the laundry. The repetitive gestures that do not require too much attention allow me to tell the Universe exactly what I "LOVE TO BE" … and I come up with new ones every day! It is a highly creative process and I love it!

Now, make the list of everything you love to "BE." It is important to use a positive phrasing for your "LOVE TO BE'S."

<u>First example</u>
Instead of saying "I LOVE TO BE free of all daily stress," use a more positive phrasing such as "I LOVE TO BE calm, relaxed and composed throughout the day."

<u>**Second example**</u>

Instead of saying "I LOVE TO BE free of any fatigue from my hectic life," use this phrasing "I LOVE TO BE energized, dynamic and enthusiastic for my daily activities."

It brings a positive dimension to what we truly desire. What we say corresponds to what we desire instead of what we do not want!

<u>**Examples and ideas to inspire you**</u>

Here is an example of my list of personal "LOVE TO BE'S"…

▶ I love to BE happy with my family;

▶ I love to BE in love with my partner;

▶ I love to BE in good terms with my friends, family and colleagues;

▶ I love to BE happy at all times;

▶ I love to BE with positive and loving people from my social circle;

▶ I love to BE perfectly healthy;

▶ I love to BE in good shape and to have energy;

▶ I love to BE balanced in my life;

▶ I love to BE in a good mood;

▶ I love to BE fulfilled with my personal accomplishment;

▶ I love to BE true, authentic, sincere;

▶ I love to BE honest, fair, unbiased;

▶ I love to BE peaceful, calm, serene;

▶ I love to BE epicurean and to appreciate the good things in Life;

▶ I love to BE surrounded by beautiful things;

▶ I love to BE comfortably relaxed at home;

▶ I love to BE grateful and happy to receive what Life offers me;

▶ I love to BE generous and spoil the ones I love;

▶ I love to BE in abundance;

▶ I love to BE rich and thriving, etc.

You can also create a much more personalized list and add more details:

► I love to BE vacationing with my partner;

► I love to BE vacationing by the sea;

► I love to BE sitting in front of a beautiful fireplace while watching a movie with my partner;

► I love to BE at ease under the sun on my patio while I read a good book;

► I love to BE happy and laugh every day;

► I love to BE to chat and laugh with my sister for hours;

► I love to BE free from time to time and enjoy myself;

► I love to BE surrounded by happy and joyful people;

► I love to BE on my own from time to time;

► I love to BE in silence;

► I love to BE meditating;

► I love to BE spiritual;

► I love to BE disciplined with my daily Yoga/Tao exercises;

► I love to BE in touch with nature daily;

► I love to BE in contemplation of nature;

► I love to BE amazed by a beautiful sunset;

► I love to BE surrounded by animals;

► I love to BE home to write peacefully;

► I love to BE working with people who work in the wellness field;

► I love to BE active to fulfill myself fully;

► I love to BE confident in my resources, potential and talents;

► I love to BE in touch with my inner capacities;

► I love to BE an artist from time to time;

► I love to BE good company for others;

► I love to BE listening to others;

► I love to BE useful to society, etc.

If you have other dreams, you can make another list with all your desires and dreams, and use the same phrasing.

That list represents your hidden dreams. By writing them down and by **keeping them to yourself**, they will come true more quickly! Make a list of at least ten hidden dreams…

<u>Example</u>

I love to BE free to do whatever I want, when I want, where I want! (Oops! It's no longer a hidden dream! Lol!)

When you know what you love, Life gives you what you need with the "Heart Connection." Make the list of **"LOVE TO BE'S"** that corresponds to the "Heart Connection."

When you connect to your Heart's desire, you connect with the great Life plane and the Universal Source. You connect especially with your "Life Mission" that manifests itself because you are guided by it. *Merci la Vie!*

♥ 2 | The Entire Universe Conspires for What We Love to "BE" ♥

"The entire Universe conspires for my Happiness and makes sure that I have everything to be happy, joyful, thriving, healthy, etc."

The entire Universe conspires for what we love to "BE" in relation to the "Heart Connection." It is not about the comparison between what you "like" and "don't like," it is about feeling the "Heart Connection" in order to live a fulfilling life more easily.

The "Heart Connection" favors full self-realization. Taking the time to focus on this aspect can transform our entire life. To think, act and feel with the Heart allows us to be in tune with the Universal Life.

This Universal Source becomes the guide for each step we take, as long as we can "BE" in tune with our Heart.

The ego (negative emotions, the mind) will always be the first one to divert us from our Heart and make us believe that there is something better than what we are feeling. The truth is, if we "diligently listen to our Heart," it is never wrong! The Heart always knows what is good for us or not.

The mind finds all sorts of "deceptive" ways to divert us from our true goals. We often know exactly what to do in order to "BE happy," to be fulfilled or to reach our life goals. Nonetheless, we lose focus because of something else in our life that entertains us or diverts us from our true needs. This subtle diversion overpowers what we truly desire.

For example, someone might wish fervently in their Heart to get their doctorate to become a doctor and help people and humanity. If they do not focus on their Heart's truth and get distracted by (unavoidable) student outings, parties, etc. they will not be able to reach their Heart's goal given by Life. This does not mean to avoid every good thing brought upon us by Life, but to come back often to our Heart's desires and to our "Life Mission" while enjoying a balanced Life!

For someone else, their main aspiration might be to enjoy life's blessings by radiating love and joy while having a great time. Careful! They will have to be wary and vigilant as not to fall in the dark sides of abuse. The lack of balance always brings consequences in life. Even if we think that what we are doing is good for us, it can sometimes lead to excess.

For example, someone who works out too much will be in an excess state that is as harmful as someone who does nothing for their health. Sometimes, "less is more," and we must find the balance in all things. Part of the reason we are incarnated on Earth is to learn about this. The first teaching from the *"Masters" is filled with wisdom and truth about Life: find "**balance**!" Easier said than done!

Most people live a hectic lifestyle without "BEING" able to stop, to settle down and to free their body, their soul and their mind. This incessant whirlwind often prevents us from making wise choices in life. We went over this topic in the previous chapter with the **Meditation Technique: How Can We Release the "Overflows"?** With this technique, we can experience an amazing rebirth in our life thanks to the "Transition to nothingness" that allows us to listen to our Heart and choose properly what is best for us.

♥ 3 | Listening to Our Heart to Follow the Best Direction in Life ♥

When we have chosen in which direction to take our Life by listening to our Heart, we already know that it will be more enjoyable because it will be rooted in our profound convictions.

♥ 4 | To Choose the Right Direction in Life, We Have Three Important Choices to Make: Option 1, Option 2, Option 3 ♥

1) Do it because you "**love the project**" using the "Heart Connection";

2) Do it for "**fun**";

3) Do it for "**money**."

In 80% of cases, people choose option 3 first in order to succeed and "be happy." The best scenario is to have two out of three options that correspond to what we truly want.

If we do it only for "money," we might (YES!) "Be" rich, but we might not be as happy as we thought we would be… If we do it for "fun," Life will put everything we need on our path for us to be happy. If we do it because we "love the project" using the "Heart Connection," Life will bring us its benefits and kindness of the Heart in order to be fulfilled effortlessly.

If our motivation is set on option 1 and 2, for the "love of the project" and for "fun," Life will guide us and put fewer obstacles in our way because we are listening to the voice of our Heart. If our true motivation is set on options 1, 2 and 3, in that order, our project is guaranteed to succeed!

For each project, you can make a list of your three options to confirm which one comes first and why.

<u>Ask yourself the following questions</u>

▶ For Option 1: How does this project makes you feel?

▶ For Option 2: How can you be motivated while having fun? How will this project bring you joy and fun?

▶ For Option 3: Can this project be lucrative and how?

♥ 5 | It's Not the Head that Controls Everything, It's the Heart! ♥

Remember that it is always the Heart that controls everything, not the head or the mind. The head can sometimes fool us or disappoint us, disorient us or change our course. However, if we let our Heart guide our head, it can achieve great things and become a valuable ally to help us reach our goals.

We have to learn to say to our mind that it works in our favor, but in reality, it works to fulfill our "Heart's" desires.

When the mind works according to our Heart's choices, Life becomes simpler and a lot less complicated. The mind's "overflow" must be released with the peacefulness of meditation and the practice of *"**Inner Peace**". If I feel an "overflow" from the whirlwind of Life or if I feel the need, I just sit and take two minutes of my time to reset and reconnect with the Heart.

You will find information about a breathing exercise on *"Inner Peace" in **Chapter XI section 2 (The Benefits of BREATHING… Prana Source of Life!)** that you can practice anywhere to feel calm and peaceful.

Meditation, breathing, silence, pranayamas, Yoga and Tao techniques of the Heart are the most powerful ways that I know to empty my mind, to recenter myself and to get back on the right path every day. You will need to be vigilant to prevent yourself from getting lost in your mind or your emotions. We must always take time to recenter ourselves and come back to the "Heart Connection," especially when we go through though life challenges. It is simple, we have to be mindful and focus every day in order to "Listen to our Heart." Careful! You have to believe it! When we stop listening to it, it can also stop talking to us, so we need to go back as often as we can and listen carefully!

♥ 6 | How Can We Practice the "Heart Connection"? ♥

The Earth's energy rises to the Heart, and the Sky's energy (the Universal energy) goes down from the head to the Heart to get us in sync with the Source of Life.

Our beating "Heart" at the center of our body is a source of Life and love. It holds an extremely powerful wisdom and

knowledge from which we can draw strength.

To think, to talk and to act constantly with our Heart is easier said than done. For those who wish to rise spiritually, it is perpetual hard work that is achieved through a constant and attentive practice.

How can we use the "Heart Connection" to permanently live in that state?

We need to "BE" appreciative of things instead of "BEING" reactive to emotions, situations or any given ideal. Learning how to "appreciate" instead of reacting to everything.

Understanding that when things do not go as planned, there is a "Purpose" for it. Behind a frustration, there often is an "overflow" that needs to be released before we can find the real "Purpose" of this event or emotion. We need to find the silver lining of a given situation that does not go how we planned it. Life knows what has to happen and plans everything to our advantage. A given situation can also happen because we need to learn something from it. We have to understand "why" an unpleasant situation happens since they all have a "Purpose," and allow ourselves to change them or to make a decision according to what we truly feel with the "Heart Connection."

When we start to **"appreciate the present moment"** and accept what actions or situations Life offers us, we get in tune with Life. "Appreciating" a situation, even if it is not what we wanted, allows us to be in symbiosis with Life's forces. This Universal Source shows us the necessary steps for our evolution and our wellness.

It leads to the discovery of the hidden opportunity behind the frustration. We then realize that the unexpected outcome of a situation is better for our well-being and that what happened might be more beneficial for us. If we think about what happened, we will realize that everything was perfect!

There is always an "opportunity" hiding behind a frustrating event … even if it is difficult to accept, everything is always perfect!

Think of a situation that had a different outcome than the one you were expecting. See and feel that what happened was for the best. Think about how the outcome that differed from what you were expecting, met an inner need or brought an important change in your life.

Remember! Everything has a "Purpose," we just need to understand it and appreciate it. That is what wisdom is all about! It seems so easy for the *"**Grand Masters**," how awesome would it be if they could "copy" their Heart and mind for all of us? LOL!

The more we follow this mindset and the more we apply it in our daily life, the easier our life becomes. Understanding our symbiosis with the Universal Source gives us new opportunities, helps us in our soul searching and showers us with abundance when we least expect it. Only when Life's blessings come into play can we acknowledge that our mind and emotions cannot rule our life at all times. The power of the Universal Source paired with the "Heart Connection" is the greatest power.

Using what is already there or "**Going with the Flow**" greatly lowers our emotional and mental blockages because we no longer react to anything and everything.

Taking "responsibility for our life" is realizing that if something unpleasant happens, there is a lesson to learn from it and we need to readjust some things or make an important decision. It can also be the "Law of Return" that intervenes.

♥ 7 | The "Law of Return" Is the "Law of Karma" ♥

The "Law of Return" is indeed the "Law of Karma."

As the wise ones say, "**Karma does not punish, karma teaches.**"

The "Law of Karma" states that everything that happens is in our best interest, even if we think otherwise! This law encourages us to act differently and to follow our true ambitions. We understand that **neglect results in consequences**, especially if cannot express clearly who we are, pay attention to our intuitions or to Life's guidance or if we cannot act in harmony with our "Heart Connection." Otherwise, it will lead to more suffering and conflicts.

Simply put, "if the Heart tells us to," it is good and positive, and if we do not feel like it … we HAVE to listen to it because "Life" tells us that it is better this way.

No matter what we do, it always comes back to us, whether it be positive or negative. We might as well do what we want in order to get the results we wished for! :))

When our emotional body is full of negativity and we keep fueling it … we can only attract what we radiate. For example, if we keep fueling our anger, our fear and our concern, it will expand and come back over and over again. On the other hand, the more we wish to radiate positive energy, the more we attract positive results and it will be beneficial for our well-being.

Every time there is an "overflow," Life lets us know!

An inevitable consequence will present itself in our life to make us realize that we need to "release" the "overflow."

A bad situation that contradicts our true desire will present itself in order to help us find the cause behind the situation. This cause, the source of all things, never comes from an outside source, but from inside of us. Each part of us reflects on our surroundings. Let us see clearly what is truly going on in our life and act accordingly to make things better.

Let us finally learn the lesson Life has for us and benefit from its understanding. It is inevitable, it is the Universal Law!

Chapter 4

Resisting = Suffering

The more we resist an unpleasant situation, such as not acknowledging that it does not serve us or suit us anymore, the more it becomes inevitable to suffer. The more we suffer, the more it indicates that we are reacting to that situation. On the contrary, when we accept what Life is giving us, no matter the reason, the suffering lessens and dissipates until it disappears. It is up to us to choose what we want!

RESIST and SUFFER

or

ACCEPT, APPRECIATE and GET BETTER!

By "resisting and suffering," we give energy to our "Ego" (see Chapter VI) that enjoys controlling our life.

Resistance, fear, etc., come from the ego. In other words, the ego is negative.

All negative attitude stems from the ego. It always thinks that everything it does for us is what is best for us.

All of that is "acceptance," "appreciation," joy, happiness, peace, calm and positivity that comes from the energy of the Heart and from the "Heart Connection" which inevitably makes us feel connected to the Universal Source. When things go well, we feel as though we were lifted by Life and gifted wings.

As if by chance (and as if chance really exists!), the greatest people of this world let themselves be carried by this great force and power of Life.

Sometimes even without knowing it, they let Life dictate what is to come and carry them to the top. They blend in Life's current and accept that their life goes one way or another because they believe that Life favorably guides them if they follow it.

When there are "walls, obstacles or resistances" that come up it is because something is not meant for us, it is a sign that Life wants something better for us, better than we ever imagined, or that there is a different direction to take.

In order to do that, we need to open our eyes and "accept" what is presented to us with no resistance or reluctance. Often, when we take a step back, we realize that some of the situations were better for us than we thought, and that the way they unfolded was better for our well-being.

Struggling and insisting on going in a direction where there is "suffering and resistance" does not heal our wounds, it amplifies them.

♥ 1 | Ask Yourself the Following Questions ♥

In which circumstances of my life is there resistance or suffering?

Is there suffering in my career, in trying all sorts of things to make it work? Is there resistance with my boss or my colleague, with my family, my partner, my friendships, my finances, with my upcoming projects? Take a moment to write it down, because writing it down makes us realize how big the situation truly is. If the resistance is in one or many of the areas mentioned above, it indicates that we are not listening to what Life has advised us to do and that we are resisting those life situations.

The "Resistance" tells us that there is something better waiting for us and that we must let go of our "walls and resistances" in order to live our best life.

Take each area of your life where you are living in resistance/suffering and write down an event that occurred where you were inspired to find an idea to fix the situation… There must have been ideas, intuitions or thoughts that crossed your mind to better the situation.

Did you do it?
Did you follow the guidance?

In most cases, we receive guidance for what we need to do to get out of an uncomfortable situation, but the resistances of the Ego (the fears) make us do things differently. When an idea or a spontaneous inspiration comes up often in our mind, at least three times, it is an inevitable sign of a great message from Life that leads us in a specific direction.

Sometimes, to follow this sign, we have to make an effort to get out of our "comfort zone," let go of our fears, of the resistances of the ego and take a real leap toward the "Heart Connection." We often put off things in the hopes that they will sort themselves out or because we are afraid to face them.

One of our biggest fears is to face ourselves, to "BE" real with ourselves and what we are going through. It is probably the hardest thing to do… to "admit" that we have to make an important decision in order to change things and truly follow the "Heart Connection."

The Ego (the mind) creates *"make believes" and takes us away from our predetermined path – the path of happiness and wellness. It is up to us to take back the reins of our life and act accordingly.

In what circumstances of my life is there resistance or suffering?

Write everything that comes to mind. Then do the opposite of what you have been doing. It will help you see certain situations more clearly and things will start to sort themselves out. For other situations where you cannot find a solution, let yourself be guided by the power of the

Heart, because the power of love heals and soothes all wounds, emotions, sadness, anger and fear.

**Stop focusing on the problems and start to
"connect with your Heart," and "accept"
that those situations are there for a reason.**

"**Accepting**" a situation does not mean "**giving up**," but accepting that we have to change the way we do, think or act.

Here is an exercise that helps to let go of any situations and quickly boosts the "Heart Connection." Practicing it helps increase our *joie de vivre* and our inner wellness.

♥ 2 | Exercise: "The Inner Sun" ♥

Description of the exercise "The Heart Connection": join your hands over your Heart in a *"**Namaste**" gesture with the "Inner Sun" breathing technique.

▶ **Put your hands over your Heart.** Breathe deeply and slowly. Picture a big bright light where your Heart is, like a big "Inner Sun" that sheds light everywhere in your body. Your body is connected to the great Central Sun that orbits around the Earth. These two Suns interact in a natural rocking motion and are interconnected. Let this "Inner Sun" grow and radiate more and more in your Heart, let it blossom at the center of your "Being."

Feel the warmth heating up your Heart, soothe your pains and heal your wounds.

▶ **Breathe in and breathe out** this great healing energy for 3 to 4 minutes without thinking of anything but this beautiful "Inner Sun" at the center of your body.

▶ Then, while you breathe, picture **the solution** to replace the resistance and the suffering. This will put Life into action to fulfill your request and help you.

▶ **Observe your results,** you will probably be surprised when you see that Life works in our favor if we take the time to work with it. We realize how much Life loves us and puts everything into place when we consciously ask for it. It makes us realize that we are part of this greater whole.

It becomes easier to say, "**The entire Universe conspires for my Happiness and puts everything into place to make sure that I am perfectly happy.**"

As your connection to this greater "whole" deepens, you will encounter more surprises along the way. The Universe will shower you with gifts and infinite blessings, as long as you are open to receive them and fully aware and "conscious" of the process.

♥ 3 | What Does the "Heart Connection" Change in Our Life? ♥

Discovering the state of "BEING" of the "Heart Connection" changes important aspects of our Life. The state of your personal relationships as well as your relationships with your family, friends and colleagues will change for the better because the "Heart Connection" allows us to make wiser choices for our well-being, our health, our family, our career and our lifestyle in general. Choices that are right and good, that are mindful of our relationships and that allow us to understand how to invest in our daily life and move forward.

The "Heart Connection" paves the way for joyful and happy personal relationships, and gives us surprises every day. We need

to "BE" attentive and find them through our daily life.

Every day can become a quest for Life's gems, for the surprises and the blessings Life offers us. You can find them every day, but in order to see them, you need to break down the walls that block you and bring suffering. These walls are built by our beliefs and our restrictive thoughts, but also by our fears, worries, concerns, resentments, angers, jealousies, rivalries, competitions, comparisons, etc. These are all states of mind that prevents us from releasing our energies or discovering the precious gift of the "Heart Connection."

These states of mind often stem from open wounds that we let fester instead of healing them. Understanding what are the reasons behind those wounds is what helps us release our inadequate and hurtful states of mind, and helps us lift the veil of ignorance. Truthfully, when we spend our energy on sufferings and life dramas, it is because in some ways, we are ignorant. Most of the time, unfortunately, ignorance and innocence mean that we do not know how to change. We then constantly repeat the same patterns that we have learned from generation to generation, through our parents, grandparents, and society as a whole. It does not mean, however, that everything we have learned is detrimental and needs to be changed or banned.

To escape ignorance, we simply have to learn to "free ourselves from the wheel of (negative) karma" that keeps us trapped in detrimental attitudes and behaviors.
We need to learn how to "transform" everything that keeps us from moving forward into "loving energy," everything

that prevents us from fulfilling our Life in order to meet our desires and true ambitions.

It is the only way to "BE" truly accomplished and discover the hidden treasures within us, such as our hidden talents and our potential for achievement. The more we are aware of this process, the more we trust ourselves. We must believe that Life will be there for us with its unconditional support and guide us through our evolution. MERCI LA VIE!

♥ 4 | "Be" in Tune With Life ♥

Sometimes being in tune with Life is not what we want, especially if it changes what we had planned for the day. However, if we decide to see it as a great and unconditional help from Life, it becomes easier to follow it. This way of thinking allows us to adapt without negative emotions or frustration because we know fundamentally that it betters our quality of life and is good for our well-being.

This anecdote of what happened in my personal life while I was re-writing these lines is a good example:

"Today I had planned to do my bookkeeping, but I didn't have the energy. It was a tough day emotionally because of the turmoil in many aspects of my life such as the passing of my father, the settlement of his estate, etc. The effort I put in finding monetary solutions tires me and all these events make me feel powerless. The last years of my father's life were tough and my major 'life transition' made it even worse. Visiting the hospital constantly, adjusting, moving my father many times because of his medical condition and then planning the funeral at the same time that I was selling my business, all while trying to find a new career path to start anew… OOF! The fast pace of all these events made me feel a wide range of emotions coupled with the sad reality of losing a parent, and losing a big part of my life after 18 years in business."

When I feel like this, I go up to my meditation room and practice some emotionally liberating breathing exercises using the evacuation method to release the "overflows." Like every other time I am not at my best, I try to let go of the situation, and take a break to do things I love. Even if I have to work, it helps me get back on my feet!

I suddenly decided to rewrite my book after a four-month hiatus. Writing always brings me joy and re-energizes me. Sitting comfortably, I started writing again. When I was rewriting my book, I listened to the spa/relaxation music channel on television. Coincidentally, a song of "***Aeracura**: Goddess of prosperity" was on (Ha! There's such a thing as a Goddess of prosperity!), followed by the songs *Close to You* and *The Day After Tomorrow…* Funny coincidence! I understood that things would change for the better the day after tomorrow, in two days! That is exactly what happened – a monetary solution came up unexpectedly…

The day of the Goddess's apparition, I had the intuition to call back a broker with whom I had already worked with. I contacted him and he informed me that he could find a solution. It surprised me, as I had been trying to find a solution for my life transition for months now. He informed me that he would update me as soon as possible.

Two days after, we were "The Day After Tomorrow" … and the beautiful Goddess "**Aeracura**" was right! I simply could not believe it … there finally was a solution! But I could only be truly happy when I would have positive feedback from the broker. I had waited all day, and sadly had no answer. I said out loud, "Aeracura, you'll have to prove that it's true if I'm to believe in you!"

After a long day of waiting I closed my computer, exited my office and cooked dinner. I was really disappointed. Shortly after, I walked pass my television that was still playing the spa/relaxation channel and I saw, written in capitals, the title of the song that was playing *Aeracura…*

I turned up the volume and heard the same song that played two days ago. I quickly understood the message! I ran toward my computer and… INCREDIBLE, but "TRUE"… I had received an email from my broker who confirmed that my monetary transaction had been approved. I did not process the news right away, I was blown away by the synchronicity of Life. It was impressive, especially since my husband and I were almost jobless and going through a "professional life transition" which did not put wind in our sails, that's for sure!

My wishes had been granted and Life made it happen quickly! I had told two days ago to *"**Aeracura**" that my request was "urgent" because she was the "Goddess of Prosperity for monetary urgencies." At that point in time, I was ready to ask any Saints or Goddesses! Lol! Imagine my surprise when, two days later, I saw the song title with her name on my television screen! As a skeptical person, I can easily say that Life gave me a lesson, **"Believe in Life and keep faith."**

In other words, when Life tells us to do something, it is beneficial to listen to it because it is always for our own good. If I had not followed Life's guidance and decided to start my bookkeeping as planned, without altering my path, I never would have seen the song titles that turned out to be synchronized with my previous requests and to be the answers to my questions. I listened and was able to regain a nice flow of energy, comfortably seated in my solarium while listening to soft music. By "listening to my Heart," I was able to reconnect with the great happiness of "Being" calm and in a peaceful state of mind while rewriting my book and finding solutions to my problems!

From now on, when Life asks me to do something, I listen carefully and **I do** these things without even knowing why I do them, because I know that Life guides me toward beneficial outcomes.

Sometimes, when an important thought comes to me at night, wakes me up and tells me to "write," I turn the lights on and get to work with my eyes half-closed, even though I would rather stay in bed. I can write non-stop for two or three hours. Why was Life telling me to write in the middle of the night?

I understood the next day, it was the perfect time to write: away from the whirlwind of Life, in silence and with all the time I need. Life knew that these conditions were ideal and that it would not have worked as well during the day. What's more, the next day, I was surprised to wake up with the same level of energy I usually have when I get a full night's sleep.

♥ 5 | Discovering the "Heart Connection" ♥

Discovering the "Heart Connection" allows us to better understand our intuitions, ambitions and *"**Divine Guidance**". (The "**Divine Guidance**" notion refers to the absolute power of the Source of Life. Some call it the strength of the Universe, Life Source or Supreme Greatness.)

I have learned overtime to listen to every intuition, inspiration and divine instruction because they are a part of the "greater whole" that helps me be truly fulfilled. Rest assured, I am far from perfect! I occasionally lose my focus and stop listening to Life's guidance. However, when I go through a destabilizing event that feeds my suffering or when something unpleasant happens, I promptly go back home! "Get back home! Come on!" Lol! … I am referring here to the "Heart Connection" home of course!

The feeling we get when we do something because of the power and strength of the Universal Source is liberating and can transform our inner self. In the next chapter, we will explore how to develop the capacity to free ourselves from the "veils" of ignorance, negative emotions or the omnipresence of the mind. They are all obstacles to our wellness and prevent us from listening to our intuitions. This liberating feeling allows us to fully accomplish ourselves.

When we follow the divine guidance, or the power of the source of Life, we do not feel like we are working or making an effort. Time flows and stops being stressful because everything happens naturally. We no longer feel time passing, we happily live in the moment.

Time becomes "timeless," as if we connect at the right time with the power of the "greater whole." We then accomplish many things for us and those around us. We altruistically, generously and sincerely help others with no animosity, bitterness or resentment.

The "Heart Connection" makes all sorts of little miracles happen in our lives, it can be surprising! We are filled with joyful moments and blessings. We are also filled with boundless Love! (The song The Heart of Aurora is playing on the television … talk about synchronicity!)

♥ 6 | Reaching a New Stage to Grow and Thrive. Reaching What We Deem Unattainable ♥

How are we supposed to trust Life when we feel that everything we strive for is not happening or does not have the expected result? How are we supposed to go on without worrying about the results? Everyday life requires tangible results. We all live in the reality of our omnipresent needs: the basic needs to make a living, to pay our bills, to take care of ourselves and those we love, to take care of our home and our possessions, etc.

Why should we limit ourselves to the emptiness?

A lot of soul-searching followed that question as well as deep thoughts about Life and the notion of emptiness, of recurrent sufferings and the fears to overcome to keep going. Suddenly, many questions/answers came to me! You will find them in the following pages…

♥ 7 | Why Are There So Many Recurrent Sufferings? Questions/Answers ♥

One day, as I was meditating in one of the most fragile and vulnerable moments of my "life transition," I could see that all my efforts and actions did not have the outcome I expected. Life talked to me, loud enough for me to hear!

Life:

"During this life transition, were you missing anything?"

My answer:

"No!"

Since Life was talking to me, I took the opportunity to ask a few questions. You will now read Life's answers to my questions. A very helpful Q&A. I wrote down the conversation with Life because, in my opinion, these answers are general spiritual principles that can be applied to everyone and to many situations, depending on what you are going through. Let's start with Life's great message at the beginning of this unique meditation…

Life:

"Look at what you truly have and be Grateful." Empty everything out, **"Repeat the following mantra and give all of your distress to Life":**

"I give you, ***God**, all my sorrows, my disappointments, my worries, my sadness, my let-downs, my distress, my tensions from life, my financial stress, my fear of losing everything, etc."

(***"God"** here refers to the absolute power of the Source of Life. Some call it Universal strength, Source of Life, Supreme Greatness, Khrisna, Yahweh, Elohim, Allah, Lord God, Jehovah, Jesus or Buddha. The name does not matter, as long as we are comfortable with it and that it means **"Supreme Greatness."** It is up to you to choose its meaning.)

My first question, "How should I move forward?"

"I cannot do it, I am exhausted, discouraged, I have no motivation or interest, how should I do it?"

Life answers:

"Release your overflows until you can feel the divine power within you."

Be like Buddha, "Stay there until you can enter the infinite possibility of Life."

My answer:

"Oof! No problem! Sounds amazing, but how long will I stay there??? Centuries?" Lol!

My second question, "What is my 'PURPOSE?'"

Life answers:

"You need goals and objectives, it is the only way to stay on course, to believe in yourself, in Life and to achieve your dreams. Your belief needs to be greater than your DOUBTS and your FEARS. You need to go through the **'Forced Transition'** of your DOUBTS and FEARS to know and experience success."

My answer:

"My 'PURPOSE' is to inspire and help people, but currently, I need to help myself first… Lol! I understand, however, that in order to succeed I need to release all the overflows and overcome my fears."

My third question, "How should I do it?"

Life answers:

"Write what inspires you and act accordingly every day."

My fourth question, "What can the suffering teach me?"

Life answers:

"Even in suffering, shadows and darkness there is light. You need to take a step back in these difficult times and look within yourself to find the light. It is the light of the 'Heart Connection' that transforms everything with its radiation.

Ask your inner light to grow within you, to transform the dark spaces that prevent you from achieving your goals or are hurting you, to transform the flaws or bad habits that are refraining you from moving forward (like how our procrastination stops us from being completely fulfilled). Ask your inner light to transform all the negativity that causes suffering and allow it to transform your pain, your fear, your disappointment, your anger or any other suffering into an energy of love and accomplishment."

My answer:

"YES! I understand that, '**even in pain, darkness and shadow, there is light**'… This book is the light that came from my journey in darkness…"

Life answers:

"Close your eyes now, feel this positive energy in your Heart, let it shine naturally and spread everywhere in your body. Relax and let the **light of your Heart** work its magic."

<u>My fifth question, "What should I ask my inner light?"</u>

Life answers:

"Humans are the only beings to have the capacity to choose … this is why it is so important to choose what we truly want because '**if one does not know which port one is sailing, no wind is favorable!**'" Remember, Life is a matter of choice, the choice to react to what you experience and go through."

Be honest with your demands, because the Divine in you is at your service. It acts for the better, based on your choices. You need to delegate, as if you were working with an assistant, and let them work, but you also need to trust them!"

My answer:

"Thank you Source of all life! *Merci la Vie!* I needed that comforting feeling, to know that I was not alone… Yes! I know we all have guardian angels looking out for us and that the divine is guiding us at all times.

Thank you for bringing me back to order and thank you for reminding me that I am a child of the Universe. That its power lives in my Heart and that each time I connect with it, my life's purpose becomes clear, that I live in happiness and joy to fulfill myself every day. I now understand that if I suffer, it is a sign from the 'Source of

Life' to help me be who I truly am and to further practice the 'Heart Connection.' Thank you! Thank you! Thank you! Gratitude!"

These answers brought me comfort and guidance.

They were not supposed to fix my life with the wave of a magic wand, but bring me back to my essence, my inwardness, my **"Heart Connection."** I realized that Life answered with techniques to recenter myself and showed me how to ask things to the Universe by staying true to my profound "SELF." It was never about precise exterior subjects, but rather about guidance in order to center myself for my well-being.

♥ 8 | The Abundance Laws Are Ever-Present ♥

The Abundance Laws are always working for us. Let's meditate on the matter and focus on the Universal Light that allows us to move forward and brings the creative energy of inspiration. In order to feel the strength and the love of the "Source of Life," we have to be able to open our Heart and to abandon ourselves to its love that heals all. Even our deepest and most disturbing fears and worries (that we all experience sporadically) need to be transformed sooner or later by this great power.

When we feel like we are on the edge of the abyss, that there is no "light at the end of the tunnel," it means that there is some cleaning up to do, that we need to let go of the "overflows" in our lives. It often means that Life has a new plan for us.

Step 1:
Find which part of your life needs to be cleansed and act accordingly. It is the first step to help your wellness, the rest will come later.

(See the **14 Liberation Techniques of your "Overflows"** in **Chapter XI**, at the end of the book.) When we feel like our life is shifting into the unknown, the nothingness, the emptiness, when we feel like little parts of us, our life, our environment and what we are used to are dying, it means that we are experiencing great inner transformations of our usual guidelines as well as a "life transition." In those moments, Life is often doing the exact opposite of what we are feeling or what we want in order to destabilize us and encourage us to act differently, allowing us to discover new horizons. **We need to act differently than the way we normally do.**

Unbeknownst to us, this "life transition" is often a sign of evolution for something better. It is an elevation process that gets rid of all the guidelines that we are used to. It gets rid of our old ways, of our "overflows," and allows us to reach the true power of the "Heart and love Connection."

It might sound nice, but when we are going through tough times, it is not so easy!

Our first instinct is not to think about the "Heart Connection," believe me, I know what I am talking about!

After going through many challenges and experiencing a number of difficult moments, or when things are not going smoothly, I do my best to come back home (the "Heart Connection") as quickly as possible.

Because this lady here does not like to go through negative life experiences! LOL!

♥ 9 | FEAR: Our Biggest Mental Block ♥

We are often scared to go through this "Forced Transition" in Life, because it "forces" us to let go of almost EVERYTHING! The fear increases our sensitivity and our fragility. This fear to abandon ourselves to the infinite power of Life and to the greater whole blocks our Heart opening.

Walls, protections and defenses are all fears we "unconsciously" put in our way to protect ourselves from the ups and downs of daily life.

Through this "Transition to Nothingness,"
Life asks us to believe and to have faith. It
asks that we let go of all our resistances, to
cleanse ourselves from them and to let the
"Heart" rule our life.

It explains why, during these difficult moments of insecurity, we protect ourselves spontaneously from certain situations, events or people. It is because we are scared of getting hurt on the emotional and affective planes. The need to spontaneously protect ourselves is legitimate. It is Life's way to spare us from some of the negativity when we need it. It allows us to focus solely our "Self" during our "Life Transition."

Unfortunately, if we cannot overcome the fears, the resistances and the blockages, we might close ourselves off and live like robots, acting out of habits and automatisms learned overtime and doing everything on principles.

However, if we see the "Transition to Nothingness" as a gift from Life that allows us to experience a "healthy evolution" of our living condition, it will become easier to trust our "intuitions, inspirations and guidance from our Heart." **Our Heart knows exactly what is good for us at all times.**

"The infinite power of the Universe" is
always guiding us and puts everything into
place to allow us to be happy and in tune
with ourselves and our heart. It is a
Universal Law.

♥ 10 | Life Transition = Life Evolution ♥

Experiencing a "Life Transition" tied with a "Life Evolution" is extremely beneficial. We must see it as a journey to better our future and ourselves instead of a process where we lose all of our bearings and our balance. This perspective changes the dynamic and general aspects of this "life transition," we will see the positive aspects of the situation as well as the gifts Life intends for us.

How should we do it?

By taking the time to make our demands to Life on a daily basis. By asking for blessings, for strength, for courage and for the faith to continue this transition.

We need to take the necessary steps to release the "overflows," to open our Heart, to let go and to accept the help and guidance.

♥ 11 | The Fear of "Getting Help" ♥

"Getting help" is also a major problem from our resistances. Many people do not truly accept help. They have learned during their childhood to do everything by themselves and to move forward in order to succeed, to be successful and to be fulfilled, or simply to get out of unpleasant situations with their own strength. They do not let themselves be guided by Life. Life teaches us with the "Transition to Nothingness" that acting this way is also a form of resistance and blockages because this behavior is motivated by deep fears. The fear of failure, of emptiness, of lacking something or of letting go.

The greatest fear is to abandon ourselves to "something greater than us," stronger than the mind and the ego.

Realizing it is part of the process.

The realization allows the Universal Source to activate the strength and the courage we need to free ourselves from the societal norms taught to us since childhood.

Accepting to be helped and to "get help" requires humility and the ability to surpass our ego that wishes to control everything… But Life knows better!

The more we become aware of the process and the more we open ourselves to receive Life's help, without resisting, the more our transition and evolution will become easy, peaceful and joyful. We learn to act based on our "Heart's guidance" that is directly linked to the Universal Source.

♥ 12 | A Comforting Mantra When We Need It! ♥

Here is a comforting mantra we can repeat to ourselves, in our mind, when we need it the most. It is one of my favorites that I repeat regularly to get in touch with the Universal Source, it is the mantra that I mentioned earlier:

The entire Universe conspires for my Happiness and puts everything into place to make sure that I am perfectly happy.

You can add any desires or intentions you want to it.
Ask what you want to the Universe!
The list can differ from the one you made for the "Love to be's."
Tap into your creativity and ask precisely what you want because…

Example:

"The entire Universe conspires for my Happiness and puts everything into place for me...

▶ to be perfectly healthy;

▶ to be in harmony with my heart's guidance;

▶ to be balanced emotionally, mentally and spiritually;

▶ to be fully receptive to my intuitions;

▶ to be able to let go easily and peacefully;

▶ to be trusting Life every day;

▶ to be open to the blessings and gifts from Life;

▶ to be shining with success and accomplishment with every action;

▶ to be financially stable;

▶ to be completely free and independent financially;

▶ to be free to plan my schedule and how I spend my time, etc."

Write down all the sentences you want on paper and keep it close and visible to allow you to read it at least once a day. Ideally, you want to read it when you wake up or when you go to bed, or both, read it at dawn or dusk, in the morning or in the evening. Reading it in the morning sets the mood for the day and reading it at night allows us to cleanse our mind, to relax and to sleep better. It also allows us to send positive energy toward our desires!

If you start to talk in your sleep, it might be a sign that your plans will come true! LOL! Fear not, repeating affirmations during the day does not mean that you will start to talk at night! Lol!

Chapter 5

The Ego's Veil

Our Ego uses all kinds of ways to keep us away from our "SELF." One of these ways is to make us believe that we do things out of generosity, obligation, responsibility or selflessness. We have to be perceptive to notice it, but most of the time, it is the ego that is acting up when an emotion comes up.

When we have negative emotions, the ego does not consider the positive outcomes.

The ego represents everything that has to do with unsettling emotions and generates negative outcomes into our lives. This is why we have to "BE" aware of our fears, our angers and all our emotions in order to recognize that **Life wants to show us something that is important in our lives.**

♥ 1 | Life Wants to Show Us Something Important ♥

Life wants us to be in touch with the strength of the "BEING" within us in order to understand that it is not up to the ego to rule our lives, but to the "infinite power of the Heart."

The Ego is positive when it serves our "BEING" and our Heart, and when it contributes to our life's organization. That is its true calling, one that is useful and necessary!

Learning to live without all of these habits and beliefs of life requires us to deprogram our life's patterns in order to find our way back to the balance in every circumstance.

As mentioned earlier, "Life often knows better than us what is good for us or not."

It always dictates the only true path… But we have to learn to listen to it in order to hear it! Usually, to clearly hear its messages, Life makes them echo louder and louder until we fully comprehend the lessons behind it.

Throughout our life, we will learn and integrate those lessons that help us to "Be centered" and to live with the "Heart Connection" at all times.

The more we do it, the more Life will shower us with its blessings of happiness, peace and love. It puts everything into place for us to be happy, even if we sometimes do not see it at first! Often times, it is during a "life transition." It is often much later that we realize how perfect everything truly was! Despite all of the sadness and suffering that this change made us go through…

♥ 2 | So, Why Not Let Life Guide Us? ♥

Life is an infinite source of goodness, like a mother taking care of her child with all her love.

It is there for us at every moment, even if we are not aware of it because of an "overflow" of suffering coming from the veil of **"ignorance"** (the ego).

Let us open up to its great power and infinite resources. The Universal Source can do everything for us because we are its children of Light.

Let us trust it, it is the greatest challenge of our lives as well as the greatest gift we could ever give to it.

Let us bathe in its love and its gentleness.

Its tenderness brings a lot of innocence and joie de vivre in our life. It is like going on a trip and just letting ourselves go with the flow, living in the moment without worrying about everything.

We just let go, live intensely and discover gleefully what Life has to offer…

Wouldn't we love to live like that all the time!

It is with its "guidance" that Life will pierce the veil of illusion (the ego) that we keep in our everyday life. It wants us to see and feel the real beauty of life, every day, at every moment.

Paradise is not up in the Heavens, but right here in our human experience on Earth.

Deciding to live this way requires constant vigilance in order to bring us back to what is important: "BEING" focused on our true needs and on our will to live without being fooled by the veil of ignorance and illusion that the ego constantly puts in front of us to make us believe that it is what is best.

Coming back to the "Heart Connection" is having the courage to listen to Life, to let ourselves "BE" guided by it and to reap the benefits.

♥ 3 | To Choose Your Heart Is to Choose Happiness! ♥

It is really beneficial to choose ourselves, it allows us to let go of an old life that no longer suits us and leaves space for a new life, one that is true to our needs. We just have to "BE" aware of this transition and ease our way into this new life!

Be certain that this Universal Mother, Life, will be there to guide us toward what is best for us … listen to it carefully, it will guide us with so much love because it wants us to be as happy as can be.

It will show us how to choose our "Heart" to be happy!

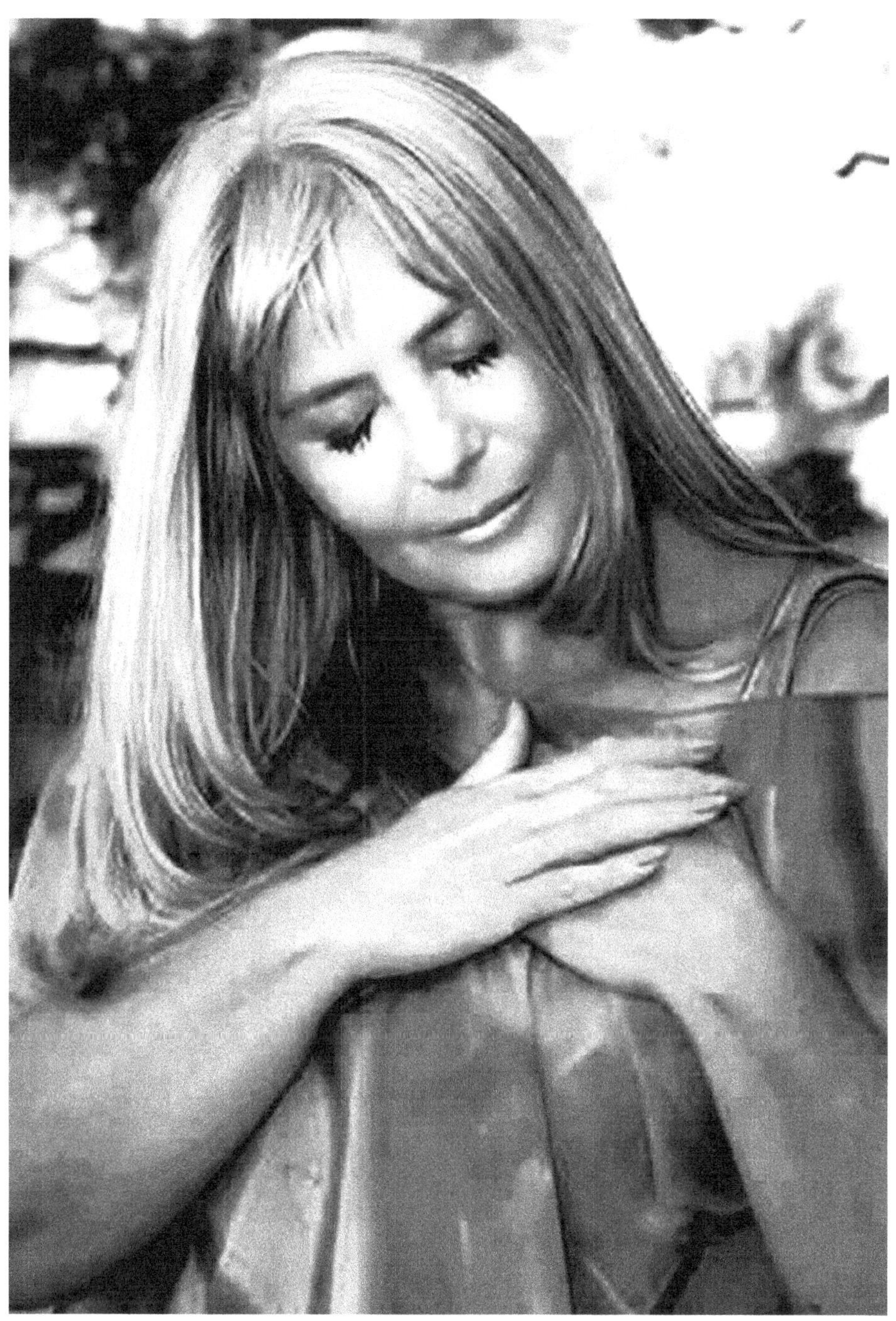

Merci la Vie !

Chapter 6

The Gift of Compassion

The gift of compassion comes from the Heart opening, from the "Heart Connection" in relation to Life's great plan of Life and from what is greater than us. We also touch this infinite power of Life with healing, love, goodness, altruism and compassion.

Because of the "Heart Connection," when something positive happens in our lives, we feel gratitude, joy and gratefulness, but even in positive situations, we can be shaken up and experience big emotions. As many wise ones say, "Humans do not like change." Change can lead to fear the unknown and to fear what is coming next. In these moments, the "Heart Connection" helps us process our emotions and go beyond the circumstances.

If something negative happens in our lives, instead of reacting to the person or the situation that disturbs us, generates fear, anger or disappointment, we must make the effort to recenter ourselves and take a few steps back. Most importantly, we need to be aware that we must quickly go back to the "Heart Connection."

We then realize that the Heart opening allows us to automatically go beyond these eventualities and be in a state of "Love for Compassion" for a person or an event.

When we are in a compassionate state, we are not "reacting" to something. We are not in a victim mindset that favors a reactive energy or a defensive state that forces us to put up our walls to protect ourselves from other people or certain situations. In the compassionate state, we become observers and, because of it, make adjustments for what suits us or not in that situation. This is how we learn to see and understand the best possible outcome from the adversity we are living and can transform it into love, even if sometimes the benefits are hard to see right away.

Each mishap happens so we can learn something about ourselves and others. You do not have to keep everyone in your life forever, once you have learned the lesson or lessons from these relationships, you can let them go.

When the "Heart Connection" is made and the lessons are learned, it means that the relationship has taught us enough and, as a result, the difficulties that it brought will dissipate.

Afterwards, if there is nothing left to learn, Life will put something else on our path. However, if the relationship is beneficial, it will pass the test of time.

When we truly are in a compassionate state, we simply become "observers of the situation" who have a great comprehension of the Heart. Being in a compassionate state means that we let go of "what does not belong to us" while being "understanding" of what the other is going through.

Having compassion does not mean to take on the role of the savior for the other. We understand the pain or the fear felt by the other person and how they can react strongly to some experiences or unknown misfortunes of Life. So, even if the person before us is defending themselves by putting up their walls, raising their anger barricades, putting on their armor, being impulsive or using inappropriate words, we are compassionate toward them. These defense mechanisms reflect a great fear, the person is doing everything they can to protect their inner self.

This emotional disruption is also true for ourselves when we spontaneously live emotional states of urgency. When we experience anger and have impulsive or violent reactions, it means that the other person or ourselves are scared of not being good enough or scared of losing something during this life event. The person is doing everything in their power to protect what is left of them.

Through all of these ordeals, we finally learn to develop compassion toward the other or ourselves instead of reacting to their distress or ours. Being scared to overreact is a defense mechanism of the ego, and the ego works hard because it always thinks it is protecting us from something dangerous.

♥ 1 | Words from the Heart ♥

Being compassionate to ourselves and others brings us love, harmony, peace and healing of the Heart.

It is just like a *"**Great Master**" in Martial Arts. When a big hit is coming, he has the wisdom to move as to not get hit and takes a step back instead of reacting and fighting back.

This does not mean to stop expressing yourself during conflicts. On the contrary, expressing your feelings with calm and caution is very beneficial, especially if we talk about our emotions with the "words from the Heart." At the same time, we are often able to put ourselves in the other person's shoes and better our understanding of their attitude and their point of view. Because of that, our feeling of compassion and of goodness of the Heart can grow.

We waste a lot of energy fighting, confronting each other and reacting to everything and anything in our lives all the time. If we put as much energy in the "Heart Connection," we would see that the path to healing is way easier and happens by itself.

By working on ourselves and on our "Heart opening," we see that things have a way to sort themselves out in Life. We realize that we are now in harmony with the people or situations that we used to disagree, fight or argue with, simply because of the "presence of the Heart."

Most of the time, we do not even need to talk to the other person. We just have to send love and say to their Heart that we understand the situation. It will get there, that's for sure, because everything is energy and we will even be surprised to see that the other person suddenly has their Heart opened too!

♥ 2 | Exercise "Words from the Heart" ♥

A quick and easy exercise that is always efficient!

Speak to the person with whom you have a conflict with your eyes closed and your hands over your heart. Have a "Heart to Heart" with them. Do it as if the person was really there, in front of you, speak to them with your "words from the Heart."

Explain how you feel, what you are going through internally and what you understand from the situation, from your actions and from theirs.

Try it, you will see the incredible results of the healing of the Heart! Just like small miracles and gifts from Life!

♥ 3 | Liberation from Conflicts ♥

Find situations in your life where the Heart's compassion would allow you to free yourself from a conflicting situation with someone. Try this exercise and, if you really are in your Heart, see the situation resolve itself.

If you are unable to forgive, at least try to understand the situation from every point of view.

<u>Example</u>
(Say this in your Heart)
▶ "I understand that you're angry because you're scared of not being good enough, I know what it feels like because I too sometimes feel like I'm not good enough."

▶ "I understand that you're rejecting me because you are scared of not being the best and to lose your spot. I know what being scared of losing your place feels like because I feel that way in this particular situation or in other situations of my life."

▶ "I understand this jealousy you feel toward me, because I know that this rivalry is a sign that you'd like to be in my place or in a similar situation. I understand all of that because I too would like to live different experiences sometimes when I look at other people's lives … or yours, even if I know it's best not to compare myself."

▶ "I understand that things are complicated for you and in your life because you're scared of losing your freedom in this relationship. I understand that you're scared of losing your freedom because I too am scared of losing mine with you."

▶ "I understand that you're scared of commitment because you feel unworthy. Being scared of commitment is being scared of the unknown, and that also brings out the fear of losing your personal freedom and/or having too many responsibilities that are hard to manage. I understand this situation well because I often think a lot before committing to any project that has anything to do with making decisions about my family, my friends or my career."

▶ "I understand that you have reasons not to do certain things because you're scared to lose your freedom of choice, to do what you want when you want, etc. I understand that because I sometimes feel that way in certain situations in my own life."

In order to free ourselves from conflict, we must be objective toward the situation and write down the sentence to the designated person or situation with the energy of the Heart. In other words, **"do as if" you were talking directly to that person**, speaking truthfully with your Heart, speak using your own experiences, begin your sentences with "**I**" … the energy will get to the other's Heart as if you were in their presence. If you are having trouble imagining them in front of you, put a picture of them close to you when you do this exercise.

If we react because of someone and we have a conflict to resolve, it is because the person in front of us is the reflection of what we **refuse to do or to "BE."** They are the reflection of what we do not accept within ourselves. We would never act like them! We forbid ourselves to act that way because of different limiting beliefs learned through society's teachings, of what is good or not, or because of values we learned from our parents.

This person allows themselves to act that way, and most of the time they do not even notice that it greatly bothers us. They give themselves permission because they feel no limitation or blockage preventing them from doing so!

By taking the "path of compassion" with the Heart opening, we benefit ourselves first and heal "our own wounds."

♥ 4 | The Consequences of Being Afraid to Lose ♥

Being "afraid to lose" is often related to the fear of losing our dignity, our freedom, our autonomy, our power, our control over others, our confidence, our courage. It is related to the fear of losing what we already have, losing money, love, attention, friendships, the fear of losing the control in our life or being scared to lose face (our credibility).

In general, "the fears" are always fears of losing something for "ourselves."

However, we can choose between the fear that keeps us trapped in the "pain and suffering" or choose "love and compassion." We can do the exercise for ourselves and our personal lives.

<u>Exercise</u>

Find an important situation that causes you trouble or brings conflict into your life and write down what you are scared of losing because of it. It will help you to make peace with this loss and become aware that this fear is not real.

Example

1) *"I understand that I react with anger toward some people or situations in my life,*

a) Choose and write down the situation (example: write the name of the people or explain the situation)

____

and I experience emotions like these

b) Write down what you are going through (example: write down the emotions that you are feeling, describe them)

____

because I am afraid of losing

c) Write down your fear (example: the fear of losing the person's friendship, their affection, their love, their presence, etc.)"

____

This is the result: (complete the sentence)

"I understand that I react with anger toward some people or situations in my life, … a) and I experience emotions like these … b) because I am afraid of losing … c)."

2) You can also "**write down the fears**" that prevent you from reaching your full potential.

For example:

"I am scared of not being good enough and not be able to prove that I am successful, etc."

♥ 5 | "Accepting Yourself" and "Accepting the Other" ♥

Since everything comes from ourselves, it is never the other person's fault or because of the other person that we experience disappointments or great let-downs.

We have to "accept" ourselves as we are, in all our aspects, strengths and weaknesses to be able to "accept" the other as they are… Especially when we know that we cannot change anyone except ourselves!

The real power of compassion is in the "acceptance of their personal choices," even if this person does not act according to our values, our beliefs or our way of thinking.

The real Heart opening is to also "accept" the other in their differences, through their choices, even if according to us they are not good, either for them, or for us. The person in front of us is not "obligated" to follow the same path as us and is maybe not destined to do the same things as us. Every path is different, and with Life experiences, we come to understand that "all roads lead to Rome!"

Besides, why did they choose the city of Rome? Québec is just as good! "All roads also lead to Québec!" Lol! On top of that, Québec is rated the best tourist city in Canada, but I must admit that I am biased, I was born there! Lol!

So, some paths are gentler and more pleasant, some are more winding and difficult than others, and some are more radical… But they all have their reason to be in order for us to attain the evolution and the freedom of the soul … and they all lead to Rome or Québec! … It's up to you!

To each their own path, when we "accept" this fact, we develop a great feeling of respect toward other individuals because we "accept" the other without judging or criticizing. The acceptation of others opens even the most closed up Hearts and favors multiple interpersonal healings.

Having real compassion toward others is letting the other "Be" completely, in their

personality, their attitudes and their life choices.

Sometimes, we think that we found the perfect solution for someone we love, thinking that it is what is best for them. This solution, however, may not be what is really best. Trying to convince them that you know what is best is a reaction from the ego that wants to control everything and thinks it knows what is best, but it is not always the case. A lot of people do this because they are ignorant or because they sincerely think that they are helping the other person, when this person, most of the time, is not even asking for any help… Sometimes, the help we provide is not really helping them and, consequently, we are not helping ourselves either. If we want to help the other person too much, they might not be able to go through their own evolution. Each person needs to set their own pace, choose with whom they want to spend their life and how they want to live. As they say, "Heaven helps those who help themselves."

This does not mean to stop being good or generous toward others who need it, but to be able to offer our help with good judgement and sometimes, in specific circumstances, only if the person is actually asking for help. We must understand and accept that the person must do some of the work themselves. Like a child trying to take their first steps, there comes a time when we must let them take a few steps alone, without helping too much. It is the only way for them to learn. They will probably bump into furniture or a table, they might fall, but they will get up again and keep learning. That is the beauty of Life!

There is always a small spark inside of us to help us move forward. When we lose our way, Life takes care of bringing us back where we need to be! *Merci la Vie*!

It is often because of unfortunate circumstances, bad decisions or some poor choices that we finally understand where to go, how to do it and when to do it. We learn from our experiences.

The more we simply accept to "BE," the more we are in touch with what Life wants for us.

It also allows us to understand what the other feels in their "BEING" and what they are really experiencing, even if their choices are different from ours.

That is "**Unconditional Love**," the real compassion of the Heart opening.

From there, there is no more resistances and blockages that prevent the bond of love from flowing between two people.

♥ 6 | Exercise on Compassion ♥

▶ Write down two situations in which you feel resistance between yourself and someone else.

▶ See and describe on a piece of paper how you can fully accept this person in their actions and attitudes, even if it does not align with your values.

It is at this moment that your connection will be free of any obstacles.

"Accepting the other" is understanding their fears, their helplessness, their angers, their hardships, their moods, their exhaustion, their deepest values and their choices while giving them the freedom to realize themselves fully as they see fit.

Trying to convince the other is like saying to them, "You are not right, but I am, I have the answers and you don't"… Which can be true, but the person must do the necessary work to find these answers themselves. It is our own ego that wishes to take control and do everything its own way through domination and power.

Being able to "BE" in "acceptation and in the Heart opening" allows us to "free ourselves" from the "grip and the power that the ego has" on us and our lives.

This is why it is so hard to go from the head to the Heart. There is a lot of "letting go" to do in between! In fact, I think that it is the "pipe" from one to the other (the neck) that makes it so hard! It's too tight! It won't go through! … It's better to laugh a little and somehow find a reason! LOL!

All of this work is done with acute vigilance toward ourselves and others, but when we reach the "compassion of the Heart," it is like heaven on Earth. A great *joie de vivre* comes from this accomplishment of the Heart.

"Accepting the other" unconditionally allows us to "accept" ourselves fully in everything that we are, with our good and bad reactions, and develop compassion toward ourselves.

Chapter 7

Diving Into the "Emptiness"

Have you ever had this feeling that you need to move on or that you need to make some important changes to your journey? But that it is hard to do because it is scary…

Diving into the emptiness hurts because we have to accept to really see who we are and discover the full depth of our personality. Accept to "BE" truly vulnerable with ourselves. By accepting to go through the difficult process that is "diving into the emptiness," we discover our great skills.

Life forces us to purify ourselves, to free ourselves from what is keeping us from moving forward and to go further into the darkness to try and touch our souls.

And just like that, this feeling of fear and helplessness will not have the same hold over us or the same meaning because we will have touched something bigger than ourselves: the strength of the Heart and the love that guides our lives even better than we can!

All of that without any resistances, blockages, tensions, expectations, disappointments, sorrow or sadness.

Dive into the emptiness at the bottom of your being and deep clean. (We will see in more details techniques to do this "deep cleaning" in **Chapter XI.**)

♥ 1 | Should We Cry? ♥

Yes! For starters, you can cry if you feel the need to cry, cry to stop attracting the energy of loss and sadness, cry to free some of the "overflows." People often stop themselves from crying because society has taught us to always show our strong side.

Life is also about expressing what does not suit us. The goal is to be able to better handle our emotions through a healthy liberation instead of holding back excessively.

In order to do so, we must free the "energy of the negative *__Thought-Form__" inside of us and stop attracting it toward us. As long as it is there, it will keep attracting events that unravel endlessly because we attract what is inside of us!

**It is a Universal Law,
the "LAW OF ATTRACTION."**

When we stop emitting the negative *__"Thought-Form,"__ we stop attracting it and reliving it over and over in our daily life.

We have to ask the Light to help us, to guide us and to purify our mind and our body. It is all that matters!

Sadness is a sign of a strong need for "Light in our Heart" and shows that it is lacking love. The important thing is to focus on the "Light of our Heart" and to cultivate the strength of the "BEING" instead of our achievements in the "DOING."

♥ 2 | No Need to "DO" in Order to "BE" ♥

Modern life forces us to "BE" in a constant state of "DOING" and to always "DO" more and "DO" faster. It creates a feeling of urgency, as if there was something missing in our life. It generates hopelessness and guilt that slows down our evolution.

The "forced transition to nothingness" and the feeling of letting go are necessary to touch the "BEING."

If things do no move by themselves, do not go any further. Do not force the future, it is best to do things by following our intuition, "Go with the flow"…

Go where your Heart is telling you to go, one day at a time, one hour at a time.

What should we do to "BE"?

By reaching the deepest part of your "BEING" through calm and silence, and by feeling the "Light of the Heart."

"BEING" = FEELING

"BEING," there is nothing else in the world that can bring as much comfort as this, not even recognition from your peers or love that others want to give us…

Because everything comes from ourselves and we must take care of our own well-being. Self-esteem comes from the "BEING" and once we touch it, **the entire Universe conspires for our happiness** in all of its dimensions.

When our mind tells us that it cannot keep going in a certain direction, we must listen to it, because it means that there is another path awaiting us.

A path that sometimes requires a "transition to nothingness" in order to experience what is best for us.

We must take that path without skipping any steps, taking it thoroughly and deeply, "diving into the emptiness" because at the end of the day, "there is always Light at the end of the tunnel!"

"The Heart leads the way" to great opportunities and helps us follow the course of Life.

The "control (the ego)" leads us where we should not go and always takes us in the wrong direction.

We must "let go" of ourselves and our resistances to follow our Heart's path.

Daring to "BE" who we really are allows our true Destiny to take place!

And now, make a list of everything that you want to "BE" to prove to your heart that you have really understood its purpose…

♥ 3 | Manifestation Exercise of Everything You Want to "BE" ♥

Make a list of everything you want to "BE" in order to realize your Life and your Destiny!

<u>**EXAMPLE**</u>

► I am here to "BE" Love;

► I am here to "BE" in tune with my Heart;

► I am here to "BE" true to my personal ambitions and convictions;

► I am here to "BE" happiness, wisdom and goodness;

► I am here to "BE" peace, calm and compassion;

► I am here to "BE" perfectly healthy;

► I am here to "BE" living in the moment;

► I am here to "BE" guided by Life;

► I am here to "BE" successful;

► I am here to "BE" fulfilled by Life;

► I am here to "BE" prosperity, abundance and wealth;

► I am here to "BE" a successful entrepreneur;

► I am here to "BE" expressing all of my talents;

► I am here to "BE" fully happy, etc.

Make a thorough list and display it on a board, on your refrigerator, in your office, in your room or on a mirror so that it is visible every day. Seeing it every day influences your thoughts. They will become one with your true essence, allowing them to manifest everything you truly want!

Yes! But you are going to tell me… "There are a lot of lists to write … which one should I pick?"

Here is a summary of the three different exercises of "lists to write down" or to "say out loud" to manifest a happy and fulfilled life with all kinds of blessings connected to our deepest aspirations and values.

1) The exercise of **Chapter III**, making the list of the "**Love to be**":

▶ Activates the "**Law of Attraction.**"

▶ Puts in motion the movement that allows our objectives to fulfill themselves. This list "speeds up the realization" of what we truly want in our life.

2) The list of **Chapter IV**, making the list of the "**Universe conspires for my Happiness…**" allows you to:

▶ Send your demands spontaneously directly to the Universe and to put creativity and originality into it.

▶ Instantly feel our bond with it.

▶ Alleviate the hardships of life by repeating this comforting sentence. It puts us in contact with the Universal Source as soon as Life becomes difficult as to feel that we are supported by a greater force.

3) The list of **Chapter VII**, make a list of "**to be's,**" like in the example above (**I am here to "BE"…**) allows us to:

▶ Be everything that we truly are and what "our Heart" radiates.

▶ Manifest what we truly want to "Be," become or improve in our life.

▶ Fill our thoughts with this list as they become one with our true essence.

It is up to you to choose the lists that suits you the most! You can also switch from one to the other … it is just as good and changes the routine!

"The entire Universe conspires for my Happiness and puts everything into place for me to be perfectly happy."

Chapter 8

Learning to Receive

"Learning to receive" does not equal control since we must abandon ourselves to the rhythm of Life, to the surprises that it has for us, to what is unknown and unplanned … to what we cannot control!

♥ 1 | Giving Versus Receiving ♥

– **Giving** is a very generous gesture … even if sometimes it means having control over someone else.

– **Receiving** is accepting that you may find yourself at the mercy of someone by being vulnerable which can scare the "ego" because it is scared of suffering and feeling "indebted."

Sadly, in our societies, we often have a hard time receiving, which prevents us from being open to "receive" what Life has in store for us!

♥ 2 | Refusing to Receive ♥

Refusing to receive is expressing rejection because we say "NO" to something that is graciously offered to us. Often, we "unconsciously" avoid receiving and we refuse what someone wants to kindly give us.

It may be a compliment, like someone saying that we are beautiful, that they like what we are wearing, etc. We must learn to simply say, "THANK YOU"! It can be as simple as someone sharing their snack with us or someone offering us a small gift … and then we tell them, "Oh! This was not necessary!"…

"Oh! You shouldn't have," etc. A reaction like this means that you are truly refusing to receive. By acting this way, we send a message to the Universe that we refuse to accept the abundance. We then attract this refusal again and again, because the "law of return" sends it back to us as a consequence of our first refusal. And we are surprised to lack abundance in our lives!

The "great givers" are often people who have a hard time receiving.

Everything in the customs of our society has taught us that we need to give to the other and open up to them… Yes! **"Giving"** is the meaning of Life.

However, we have not learned to **"open ourselves up"** in order to **"learn to receive."** If we did, we would look like self-centered people who only think about themselves.

♥ 3 | What Is "Learning to Receive"? ♥

"Learning to receive" goes far beyond the social principle. It is to be able to **open up** to what Life wants and what is best for us.

It is to learn to open up and welcome the graces and blessings of Life, to be able to recognize them in the smallest details, sometimes so small that we are not even aware of them.

"Learning to receive" is a difficult process to learn for the ego because it is used to control everything by "giving" in order to be loved by others.

"Learning to receive" means learning to receive what Life gives us and open up to it. It is receiving the gifts from Life, ideally without wanting or expecting anything in return, to have no expectations from anyone or anything and without feeling obligated to return what you have received, preferably without experiencing guilt! Oof! Not so easy! To get there, we must free ourselves from the good manners society has instilled in us! However, if we sincerely thank the person who is giving without feeling obligated to do so or just to be polite, the "bond of the Heart" will be multiplied because this gesture will be considered pure and true.

When people accept our gifts, they cannot reject us, because we usually give to the people we love and we know that they will appreciate this nice gesture and generosity. In a way, we unconsciously protect ourselves from rejection.

"The act of giving" is first and foremost a gift to ourselves because of how good we feel when we prepare the gift, when we wrap it, when we decorate it, etc., all while thinking of how happy the person who will receive it will be. The return of the goodness is already there, simply because we are in a state of gratitude when we are preparing to give.

All of that is multiplied by the joy we feel when we give generously, especially since we sometimes give what we would want to receive!

"Gifting's bliss" is the joy we experience when we celebrate with the person we have spoiled with unconditional love. The motion flows both ways, we spoil ourselves as well as the other!

That is why giving sincerely feeds our soul and our Heart. Awesome!

Why did society teach us to give first? To do this great gesture of selflessness? To simply "BE" able to open up to receive is a gift to ourselves!

"Learning to truly receive" is not part of our own natural education. We are frequently driven to go to the other first, to go outside ourselves in different aspects of Life instead of looking inside ourselves and practice the "Heart Connection."

♥ 4 | "Learning to Receive" When We Need Help ♥

"Learning to receive" when we need help requires humility and requires us to accept that others can truly help us with gestures of love and compassion. It means to let ourselves be vulnerable and to be vulnerable with others. Most of the time, unfortunately, a lot of resistance from the ego hinders the process in its essence and its purity. The ego often wants to show that it can do it, that it does not need anyone else, that it can do everything on its own. It resists the possibility to "receive" a real "gift from the Heart." It is a paradoxical process from our Heart. And yet, all human beings look for and need this love!

"Learning to receive" when we need help forces us to surrender to the fragility of our "BEING" and makes us realize that we sometimes are in true need of receiving.

The need to have someone to comfort us and listen to us, someone with whom we can express our disappointment and sadness, someone who is there, present, and who can help us with our internal hardships.

"Learning to receive" asks from us that we open up to ourselves and to our Heart honestly. It allows us to get out of the ego's illusion that makes us believe that we have power, that we are strong, and that we can decide what we want to do with our lives up to the smallest detail.

"Learning to receive" really requires us to "let go" of our expectations, of our hopes that we have for others and of events in our Lives.

♥ 5 | "BEING" in the State of Receiving ♥

"BEING" in the state of receiving is welcoming what Life brings us without having to control everything in order to be satisfied. It is learning to satisfy our need for love through inner feeling because it is the only way to receive the "Gifts from Life."

Yes! The gifts are what Life has to offer us and what is best for us! Everything comes from within and goes out in the world, even the "Art of Receiving!"

We cannot receive if we are not inclined and opened to goodness, kind gestures, attentions and love from others and from Life. The slightest feeling of guilt destroys the essence of this divine sensation of wellness. Receiving without guilt, and feeling that we truly deserve it is often difficult!

In our life, we cannot always go in the same direction or always "Give," it is why we often find exhausted people who "gave too much" of themselves in their work, to their family or to society in general that always expects more from everyone.

There has to be a meaning in receiving that we need to learn in order to live a balanced life. This requires, among other things, an open attitude toward ourselves. Taking the time each day to go inward and not only focus our energy on external things.

Time for silence, to stop, meditate, pray, come back to our roots and slow down the pace of Life that gives us what we need when we need it… Time to feel the "little gifts and miracles" of Life even more … in order to "BE" in a receiving state!

This whole process creates a major change in our lives. Our social circle, our family, our friends and our colleagues perceive us differently and think that we're changing. On the contrary, we're becoming stronger, but we are the only ones noticing it at the beginning of our transformation process.

Afterwards, our radiance and our freedom of "BEING" are the reflection of this majestic transformation. People are going to notice this beautiful energy from Life that flows freely through our feelings and through our spontaneous Heart spurs, a balance of giving and receiving. Learning this balance is a great challenge of life.

Solely "BEING" selfless, like society constantly asks us to, has created a great lack regarding the true needs of the "BEING."

Sadly, it brings a lot of dissatisfaction, frustrations, disappointments and a lack of something because we constantly "Give" ourselves to everything and everyone. This feeling of loss always grows bigger, especially when we constantly want to "HAVE" more or desire more in our life. We have to give again and again, give and give ourselves in order to "HAVE" more. It is a never-ending cycle that brings us nothing in the end.

The only thing that matters is our true need to feel the "love from the Heart" that brings and creates everything in our life. It is the only way to accomplish ourselves and "BE" happy. "Listening to our Heart," "giving" and "learning to receive" is what Life wants and what is best for us.

♥ 6 | "The Art of Receiving" ♥

"Learning to receive" is also receiving in a way that we did not necessarily wish for. It is to surrender to Life and how it does things for us in a different way than we had expected. It is to accept and see that Life takes a different path than the one we had in mind in order to guide us toward our well-being.

Life knows better than us what our heart and our soul "truly" needs. It knows way more than the filter of our "Ego" that always wants more and for everything to go its way.

"Learning to receive," is accepting to "open up to receive" all the gifts that Life has for us, no matter what they are.

The more we are open and pay attention to all the little attentions from Life, the more we attract good things. Finally, we realize that we are filled with abundance every day! Every night, write down what you have received that day, you will see, the list will be longer than you expected!

The "Art of Receiving" is no longer an expectation, but an amenity!

Chapter 9

"Being" in Touch With our Dreams

"BEING" in touch with our dreams is another option that guides us on our Life path and lets us know what we need to do and how to do it. Feeling, early in the morning, the overall emotion of a dream and interpreting it with what is going on in our life is giving us extra information on guidance and our role on our Life path.

The "Ego" cannot infiltrate dreams. When we are sleeping, the Heart automatically connects to the "soul's mission" without the "Ego" interfering. This is why the information we receive in our dreams are true and precise.

♥ 1 | The Interpretation of Dreams ♥

Like everything in the "Heart Connection" process, we must take time, only for a few minutes when we wake up, to remember how we felt in one of our dreams.

We can interpret it with what is going on in our life while discovering what Life is trying to tell us.

A little while ago, I had the pleasure of hosting my radio show about "The Art of Living a Healthy Life." I spoke about my "Health favorites," healthy products and the experience I acquired in the wellness field throughout the years.

After my show, another host took the air, she was a "specialist in Dream analysis" who has been a leading expert in the field for 30 years and has written 17 books on the subject. She invited me on her show and I invited her on mine to talk about her extraordinary dream analysis technique.

Her name is ***Nicole Gratton**, you can hear the radio show on lartdevivreensante.com.

♥ 2 | Dreams and the Guidance of the Heart ♥

During the radio interview, Mrs. Gratton explained how to make a dream postulate and how to make requests before going to bed in order to get the maximum information from the work done for us during the night.

The next morning, by taking the time to feel the effect of an important dream, we adjust to the guidance of our Heart and our soul, which allows us to find solutions to different situations in our life.

This also guides us in the right direction for the day or for the following ones…

To "BE" listening to our Heart makes everything easier in our life.

But in order to do so, we must "BE" able to listen to our Heart, to let it guide us... It's up to us to decide!

Life can also guide us and contact us in our Heart, our soul and our spirit during the night. It is up to us to take advantage of it! *Merci la Vie* for this free and additional gift that can make our Life a lot easier!

Sweet dreams!

Chapter 10

The Origin of the "Overflow"

The "overflow" of our life comes from all the ongoing efforts that are done to fulfill ourselves, to succeed, to be loved, to be liked by our colleagues, our boss, our family, our spouse or ourselves.

Notice if you do something or if you force yourself to do something without enjoying it. Write down this "thing to do" that you impose upon yourself and schedule in your calendar that is already full of responsibilities. A nagging obligation that adds to this big "to-do" list… This is the list of "I must" that we will see later.

Notice and feel this immense weight within you caused by the mere thought of this list, how it holds you back and stops you from moving forward because of how heavy it is, because there is "too much to do"…

♥ 1 | The "Forced Transition to Nothingness" ♥

The "transition to nothingness" is mandatory to be reborn and to take a new direction in our evolution, toward the direction we want for our life. If we want to evolve and start to take steps in that direction, we must inevitably get rid of what used to be, of the prior blueprints and of the former *"**Thought-Forms**" that are working against us and no longer align with who we are in order to move toward a new life.

During this "transition to nothingness," it is possible to suddenly realize that we are no longer aligned with certain values that used to be fundamental in our lives.

Our old ways cannot follow us where we want to go and are no longer viable.

In this new life, our values change, our behavior changes and the way we think evolves in the process. These stages of change destabilize us to our core. At a certain point, we might not even recognize the person we once were.

We must understand that in order to evolve it will be necessary to "let the old die and be born anew." Only the essence of love and light will remain engraved in our Heart.

This great radiating energy is always there to guide us and to help us build new things in our lives. Sadly, we all tend to hold on to what leaves our lives and on what leaves and does not serve us anymore.

It is better to focus on the **renewal energy that wants to build itself bit by bit and makes us act differently.**

Life guides us to release the "overflow" of what used to be while opening doors for our new direction in life.

That is why we all go through an unsettling and difficult period during this process. Like a child learning how to walk, they sometimes fall, but then get up, they walk and run with a big smile on their face! They continue to move forward because they know that they are protected, supported and encouraged by their parents and their loved ones. Children do not ask themselves questions, their energy stimulates them to get up and try again. This also comes from the "great inner strength" (which we all have!) that motivates them to go further. They might not realize it, but Life guides them step by step.

It is the same thing for us. The more we feel this "great strength" that protects us, supports us and guides us, the more we will move toward the unknown of our destiny confidently.

We will then connect more easily to the infinite power of the Heart. It is an aspect that we have lost over time. As for children, they do it naturally.

♥ 2 | Why Are the "Overflow" Reservoirs Overflowing? ♥

We must know that sometimes, even if we are trying to "Be" positive, to make efforts to be fulfilled and to succeed as we used to, we will hit a dead end if the "overflow" is not released. The more the "overflow" reservoirs fill up, the less Life is able to bring great things to us. It becomes impossible because there is no more space for the blessings of Life.

The "overflows" of our life create defensiveness, resistance, shackles and armors all around us. It creates rigidity, density and heaviness that prevent us from seeing the "overflows" in many areas of our lives. In these moments, there is no more fluidity flowing from the source, even the ongoing pace of Life bothers us because there truly is an "overflow" of everything.

The more we try to escape these "overflows" that we do not want to see because we are constantly in the whirlwind of Life and are asked to do things for everyone and everything, the more these "overflows" catch up to us! It prevents us from seeing inward because we direct all our energy outward, for others and for work, for the must-have career, the need to be productive at work, more efficient and more productive. This is how we forget to connect to our inner self, to our essence, to our Heart.

These "overflows" constantly add up without us noticing that, in all these "overflows," there is an "overflow" of things that do not resonate with us and must leave our lives. This inevitably activates the flooding of the reservoir of "overflows."

In the end, we would be like a pot boiling over! Once this pot is freed from these "overflows," we will start to feel better, regain a balance in our lives and have projects that better match our deepest aspirations.

Take the time to fully touch these "overflows," feel them, cry them out, breathe them out, evacuate them, transmute them… It is the only way to be able to empty yourself, to free yourself from the heaviness of the anxieties, the worries and the fears that hinder your well-being and your *joie de vivre*. It is the only way to fill your reservoirs with love, renewal, light, a new consciousness, new values and new directions in Life.

♥ 3 | "BEING" in the "I Must" ♥

"BEING" in the "I must" is the result of a lot of these "overflows" that we experience in life. When we force ourselves to be in the "I must," it represents a responsibility that we force upon ourselves. This creates a great turmoil in our lives because our primary motivation comes from our head instead of our Heart.

If we experience too many emotions stemming from "I must," Life is obviously trying to make us understand that we are going against our deepest aspirations and motivations.

These emotions are activated by our culpability that forces us to do things in order to feel fulfilled, and it is often to make other people happy, such as our boss, our spouse, our family, society, etc. We then become motivated by this fear of not being loved, appreciated, seen or respected. Whereas the opposite happens if we choose ourselves, and with this simple gesture, we motivate others who are also learning to do the same.

Choosing ourselves and respecting our deepest motivations bring back our vital energy and make our Self Love grow.

We become invincible to external manipulation and the hold it has on us. Great freedom comes from the victory of choosing ourselves in order to listen to our "true" Heart desires. It does not matter what others think. **If we respect ourselves, others will inevitably respect us.**

If, on the contrary, we force things against the desires of our Heart, Life will send a "roller coaster of emotions" our way in order to make us understand in which direction to go, which is the way to our Happiness.

What really matters is to be conscious and completely open to these signs sent by Life in order to make a decision – the right decision – for our well-being.

When there is agitation in our soul, it is a sign that we must look inward to see if what we are "experiencing and doing" truly corresponds to what "we want" or to what we have to do right now.

Do we have to go through the whole "I must" list or do we have to "listen to ourselves"?

When the strength of Life activates and flows freely, a lot of little miracles happen and things sort themselves out.

To our surprise, our list can even be done sooner than we thought, quickly and easily, simply because we did not force ourselves to complete it!

As mentioned in **Chapter IV**:

Resisting = Suffering

We must know how to "let go" in order to "BE" listening to our Heart. When we surrender and listen to what Life has in store for us and trust that it is what is best, it opens the Way to our true fulfillment.

Trusting that Life puts what is best for us on our path often surpasses the beliefs and the behaviors we have learned since childhood as well as the judgement we may have for certain situations. We often do things and make choices according to habits or routines because this is the way we have been doing them all our life.

When we need to stop acting a certain way out of habit or familiarization, or because of the automatic "I must" that we are conditioned to feel, Life sends us a "powerful signal" to unsettle us and make us realize what our "BEING" truly desires.

As we are completely overwhelmed, we have no choice but to stop and feel what is best for us. We have to make our list of "I must" according to how we feel inside and by listening to our intuition and our Heart instead of following a list of "I must" (which is made by the mind, our beliefs or the way we were conditioned to think most of the time). Silence, calm and peace bring clear and precise answers on the decisions we need to make and the best choices to make in order to write a list of "priorities of the Heart" to "BE" happy. The more we let ourselves be guided by Life, the more Life gives us gifts of joy, happiness, abundance and prosperity.

♥ 4 | The Guilt Behind the "I Must Do This or That" ♥

The "I must do this or that" that are most often than not self-imposed through our conditioned automatisms are the reflection of the guilt that we carry.

Example

A cab driver in a metropolitan area who forces himself to pick up more than five people every hour because he has a quota to meet may feel guilty if he does not reach his goal. The "I must" is detrimental to him because, by acting this way, he refuses and does not accept that providence sends him everything he needs for his well-being at all times. What is he trying to achieve by forcing himself to produce, by feeling all this anxiety, these worries and the culpability of not reaching his goals? Why does he force himself to increase his responsibilities through "I must"?

Sadly, his attitude prevents the possibility that the best situation may present itself to him in the respect of the acceptance of who he is. Imposing "I must" on himself creates harmful feelings for his well-being and is not very beneficial for his own peace.

♥ 5 | Exercise of "I must" ♥

Make a list of at least 10 things that you "must" do… "I must" do this, that, etc.

We will see later how to transform them … but make the list right now, take a moment to write them down, it will only take a few minutes because you know it very well, the list of "I must!" This infamous "to-do" list!

The heaviness that you feel, all of these "I must," is caused by the "overflows" created by the list in the moment. It is an "overflow" of build-up tiredness and efforts made to reach a goal. It is a goal that you want to reach, but have not reached, simply because it may not be the best time for you to do so, there is already "too much" for now…

There is a "right time" for everything. Life knows exactly when to time everything to ensure that it goes smoothly and joyfully. If it does not happen, it may simply be because this thing (that seems very important to you) "is not or may no longer be a part" of your path in the immediate future.

♥ 6 | How to Transform the List of "I Must"? ♥

The list of "I must" that you wrote down earlier may be related to things that you really want to achieve and that you, most of the time, like to do, strange huh! Yes! These "I must" are usually actions that we like to do, but only if we have the time for it and the energy to complete them. Because of our accumulated "overflows" and lack of time, these things can become quite heavy and burdensome. We must first release these "overflows" in order to be able to transform our list of "I must."

Most of the time, we do not see when or how we could go through the whole list of "I must," because our schedules are already overloaded with daily and mandatory obligations. All of these "I must" do not add fun to our schedule, so they become a burden and weigh on our consciousness. We cannot live in the moment peacefully and listen to our intuitions. However, as it was said before, there is a right time for this infamous "I must" list, and when the time comes, there are tips to help us accomplish it…

If you take the time to replace the sentences "I must do this or that" with "**I will happily and joyfully do this or that**," you will see that your list will change and transform because it will now be full of the true desires of your Heart instead of a feeling of obligation. You can even add your own touch of creativity to these actions of pleasure and happiness, and you will no longer feel that you "must" do it! Your "to-do list" will become a "love-to-do list!"

<u>**Example**</u>

"I must clean my house" is changed for: "**I will HAPPILY and JOYFULLY clean my house with my favorite music.**"
Result: the feeling of "I must" disappeared!

You will see that your thoughts will be quite different and, miraculously, your list will be made at the right moment, just like magic! The heaviness of the "I must" will be transformed into a stimulating and joyful project. Try it out! You will see how it changes the dynamics of your life. Instead of feeling "burdened with things to do," you will feel moments of pleasure and happiness as well as a great "sense of accomplishment!"

Well, now, it is my turn. "I must" clear my mind of all of my weekly "overflows" in order to be ready to listen to what Life has in store for me! LOL! … After a long week, a good Yoga/Tao session is a remedy I like to release the stress of a busy life!

So I change my sentence, "I must release my weekly overflows" with: "I am going to release the weekly overflows with an amazing relaxing session!"… Such a different sensation!

Of course, there are a lot of other useful techniques to discover (in the next chapter) to release all these "overflows" of daily life. I alternate between them because I like the balance brought by this variety of tools that benefit my well-being!

Chapter 11

Fourteen Techniques to Release the "Overflows"

Do you ask yourself:
— How can I purify and transform my "Overflows"?

— How can I deep clean my emotions and my spirit's repressed energies?

— How can I clear out all of the blockages with the Light of the Heart?

Here, you will find fourteen different techniques allowing you to release all of the "overflows" of your life, empty them and purge them.

Purging all the "overflows" and all the blockages every day allows us to feel the vibration of the Heart, to have a better intuition, to "Be" centered, to feel the guidance of Life and take the right direction that leads us to fulfillment and happiness. We can use one or many of these techniques as tools to fill ourselves up again with joy, love, trust, peace, calm, serenity, faith and happiness.

"The entire Universe conspires for my Happiness and puts everything into place for me to be perfectly happy."

However, we must be aware of the importance of cleaning out our inner self every time it is necessary.

Here are the techniques to empty the "Overflows" that we will see in this chapter. **You can pick one or many, according to what suits you the most!**

<u>Here is the list</u>:

1) Meditation

2) Breathing

3) Yoga

4) Writing

5) Fire

6) Water

7) Inner Cures of Wellness

8) Tao

9) Massages

10) Saunas

11) Exercice

12) Food

13) Silence

14) Order

♥ 1 | Meditation… The Best Stress Reliever! ♥

… and the best way to release our "overflows"!

We can purify our *"**Thought-Forms**" with **MEDITATION** by calming our mind.

What Is the Purpose of Meditation? What Are the Benefits?

You probably have heard these sayings often: meditating can help boost creativity, increase energy, reduce stress and even have an impact on our ability to concentrate and succeed. From business men and women to artists, many are interested in it. For me, it had the same impact on my mind than the one **Yoga** and sports have on my body: it made me stronger and more flexible.

A lot of studies show that meditation is a powerful weapon against stress (30% to 40% decrease after a month of practice). Meditation brings a significant diminution of stress and anxiety, boosts the immune system, increases the antibodies by 20% to 30%, stabilizes the emotions, helps with concentration and attention span, brings great inner peace, serenity, more positive feelings, happiness, love and well-being to your life.

What Does It Mean to Meditate?

If you are having a hard time making a decision or you simply are stressed out because of work, meditating can help you find peace and create a distance between you and the things that are stressing you out. Then, things can become a lot clearer in your mind. We all dream about finding our inner peace, finding silence and being in touch with ourselves as often as possible. Meditating allows us to get back to a state of inner calm and puts an end to the stress and anxiety that constantly troubles our day-to-day lives. When we calm down, we find an emotional balance. We can usually feel the calming effect of meditation after the first session.

The power of meditation comes from the fact that we are connected to our inner being, that we develop a connection to "ourselves." It is only within ourselves that we can find deep relaxation, calm and true love. These qualities and states of being cannot come from money, social recognition or any other external thing. Fundamentally, we know this, but we often forget.

What Is Meditation? What Is the Goal?

Meditating means "to become a witness," to simply observe our thoughts, emotions, physical sensations and the "overflows" that are inside us.

"MEDITATING" is a process that allows us to find ourselves again, as often as possible, in a "RIGHT HERE, RIGHT NOW" state of mind, to be in the power of "THE PRESENT MOMENT."

It also allows us to "**Let Go**" and accept that thoughts are like birds flying across the sky. If every time you meditate, you see your favorite movie in your head, it means that you are daydreaming a little too much and that it is time to come back here, in the "**Present Moment**"!! Meditating means "observing," but you do not have to watch the whole movie! Lol!

We all wish some days that we could live in "The Sound of Music," the Great Love, happy moments filled with tenderness as presented in this beautiful movie and classic of my youth with Julie Andrews! Such a beautiful movie that inspired me so much to live a happy life with my husband and to make of each little moment, as often as possible, a moment of happiness, because it is these moments that make up our whole lives.

I have made it a mission for my love life!

And now, when I meditate it is "The Sound of My Own Music" that I hear, that I see, that I observe, I let go to feel it better … and once it is done, the Heart adjusts itself and takes action, if needed, to make a healthy improvement.

HOW TO MEDITATE? WHERE TO START?

You can meditate almost anywhere: in the bus, at work, in a waiting room, in your living room, when you are washing dishes, taking a bath, before going to bed, a little 10 minutes each night before sleep! Everything can be meditative: a smell, a sound, music, a candle flame, a mental image of a tree, the sea or anything that inspires you.

What matters is your concentration, the attention you give to your object of meditation and your intention to empty your mind of the "overflows."

However, if you suddenly say during your meditation practice: "I regret that I have not started meditating sooner!" … it means it is time to "come back!" It is the same thing if you tell yourself: "This is it, I am completely present in this meditation" … there it is too, it means that you were gone and went back to square one! Lol!

If you want good results, you have to regularly and diligently practice! Start by doing two to three minutes per day, it will be easier when you get to ten minutes.

AND THE RESULTS?

Meditating educates the mind and allows it to develop a number of good qualities like being more present of what we are doing in the moment or to listen to our body and to our profound ambitions more. It can also have a great impact in every aspect of our life!

What meditation brings to each person is different. For my part, it brought the ever-growing need to focus on the "**present moment**," to recenter myself a bit more every day and to release the sometimes relentless "overflow" of the whirlwind of life.

When you are meditating, are you asking yourself this question:

"Am I wasting my time?"

If you think that "MEDITATING" is a waste of time, remember how important it is to create, every day, little moments to cultivate spaces of serenity and inner peace, because they are very beneficial.

The state of calmness created by meditating is far more beneficial for our well-being than the one brought by money, prestige, honors or knowledge. Meditating also releases us from our "overflows" of daily life. It is up to you to experience it! You can discover the joy of being focused on what is, without judgement, the joy of freeing yourself from your worries or to foster a desire, the joy of simply feeling alive. Moreover, it is really "**EASY**" to meditate! Start now, the results could surprise you! After, if you feel good, sensitive, open to others, calmer and more relaxed on the inside … it means that you are doing great!

♥ 2 | The Benefits of Breathing… ♥

PRANA SOURCE OF LIFE!

We can purify and change our thoughts, emotions and feelings by **BREATHING**.

Those of you who love **Yoga**, be aware that the "**Pranayamas**" breathing techniques are powerful tools to release *"**Karmas**". They purify our energy channels, the "**Nadis**" and our energy vortex, the *"**Chakras**".

WHAT IS PRANA?

*"**Prana**" is the "**Strenght of Life**," the vital energy that we all need in order to feel good. The Hindus call it *Prâna*, the Chinese and the Japanese *Qi*, *Chi* or *Ki*. We live because of it and through it.

Without Prana, the physical body and life in general would not work properly. We absorb the Prana by breathing. The Prana is found in thousands of small particles in the air. Prana is the *"**negative ions**" in oxygen. It has been scientifically proven that there are many microscopic particles of Prana in the mountains, by a lake, by the sea and in very abundant quantities after a storm of heavy rain.

The atmosphere near a cascade, a beach or a forest makes them the places with the highest level of ionization for a complete and natural balance. The calmest and most refreshing regions of the world are charged with billions of negative ions.

The more a place is charged with negative ions, the more vital energy there will be and the more Prana particles there will be.

Location	Number of negative ions per cm^3 (natural presence)
Near a cascade	50,000
In the mountains	8,000
By the sea	4,000
In a forest	3,000
In the countryside	1,200
In the city	200
In an office	20
In a car	14

You can find the original table here [in French]: http://www.sens-original.com/_medias/ionsnegatifs.jpg

► The quantity of negative ions per cm^3 of air can go up to 8,000 in the mountains, 4,000 by the sea, 3,000 in the forest and 1,200 in the countryside compared to 200 negative ions per cm^3 in the city … and only 20 in an office!

► The norm for the human body is from 1,500 to 2,000 negative ions per cm^3 in order to have a good vital energy level on a daily basis. To have perfect health, it would be best to live in the suburbs, in a forest (ideally in the mountains) or by the water.

▶ The *"**negative ions**" enter our body through our skin and lungs and are then carried in the whole body through our blood flow and our energy channels.

So, when we feel like we really need to "get some fresh air" it is because it really is time to go outside, in nature, and fill up on Prana! The good news is, the negative ions are actually positive!

HOW IS THE PRANA BENEFICIAL FOR THE BODY?

We take in the most Prana by breathing, that is why "**pranic breathing**" in Yoga is so important. The Prana flows in our body by thousands of small channels called "**Nadis**," we have 72,000 in total. These small channels carry the Prana through our whole body and help stimulate our vital energy. The Yoga and the ancient breathing techniques that come from the wise ones help us to cleanse and release these energetic currents from our body in order to let the energy of Life flow freely through our body, our muscles, our arteries, our organs, our bones, our blood flow, etc.

The Asanas (Yoga Poses), that are done before breathing, activate our blood flow, open up the capillary and the "**Nadis**," allowing the oxygen and the negative ions to spread in the body. So, the negative ions (the one that are good for us) enter the blood flow and create a positive energy for the body by stimulating our vitality, which favors a positive attitude by producing serotonin (the Happiness hormone).

A good level of Prana in the body increases the energy levels of our health capital, our well-being and our immune system.

Depriving our body from this positive Prana energy causes a lack of vitality, fatigue, laziness and cellular aging. It can make us depressed, irritable and increases the number of "overflows."

The higher the "Prana level" is in the body, the calmer, more positive and enthusiast the mind is.

If we are worried, tensed, uncertain or if we have to deal with conflicts or negative situations on our life, "**BREATHING**" seems to be the best source of Prana, which will help us to deal with all these situations.

WHAT ARE THE BENEFITS OF BREATHING?

People only use around 30% or their lung capacity. Our breathing reflects our state of mind. For example, if we are angry, our breathing will be shorter, faster and irregular. If we are calm, our breathing will be longer and relaxed.

By paying attention to our breathing, we can change something unpleasant into a feeling of well-being. All we need to do is take the time to stop and breathe!

Most breathing techniques, called "**Pranayamas**" in Sanskrit, focus on lengthening the duration of the breath in order to increase the vitality through a longer oxygenation and a greater energy intake provided by the negative ions.

Prana means "Source of life"

and **Yamas** means "Filling the body."

Together, they mean "**To fill the body with the source of Life.**"

Every conscious breathing technique puts the energy in the air (*"**negative ions**") at three different levels:

▶ **The physical level**, it promotes the elimination of toxins, tissue regeneration, stimulates healing, it releases tension in the body, awakens sensuality and helps to have a more fulfilling sexuality.

► **The emotional level**, these techniques calm the nervous system and help us develop a better body/emotion/thought synchronicity.

► **The mind level**, the two cerebral hemispheres are balanced, our mental clarity is improved which helps with our good judgement and promotes a positive problem resolution.

A QUICK AND EASY BREATHING EXERCISE

There is a breathing exercise that I particularly love. Breathe in deeply to fill up your lungs and try to keep as much air in as possible while thinking about the word **"Peace."** After, when you exhale, visualize and spread the feeling of well-being through your entire body.

► Repeat this five times. It's simple and effective! Do it right now and see how good it feels!

► You can do the same thing with the words **"Health"** or **"Vital Energy"**… Then you fill up on a good dose of Prana! … And an even greater one, if you are in nature!

The level of vitality present in blood, the **"Nadis"** and the individual cells determine the condition of the human body. So when we develop the capacity to increase the Prana in our bodies and in our cells, we gain harmony and health in our lives, both at the body and at the mind level. You are guaranteed to be relaxed, healthy and to return to your roots!

WHAT IS THE IMPACT OF THESE NEGATIVE IONS ON SLEEP?

On a neurological level, the *"**negative ions**" have a positive impact on depression, anxiety, stress and states of panic.

The negative ions (that are positive!) promote peace and relaxation, getting us ready for a good night of sleep.

Experimentally, as reported by ***Dr. Hervé Robert**, after 30 minutes, an ionizer diminishes the frequency and the amplitudes of alpha waves. This diminution happens just before sleep. The ionization allows us to go to sleep faster. The Pranic effect of the negative ions stimulates a restorative sleep and the complete rejuvenation of the body.

♥ 3 | Yoga… A Healthy Lifestyle! ♥

Yoga releases tensions in the muscles caused by stress and "overflows."

THE POWER OF YOGA

Yoga is an amazing lifestyle to release stress and daily tensions. It helps with nerves, calms the mind, boosts the immune system and gives us vitality!

"Practicing Yoga" helps with chronic fatigue, muscular tensions, depression, panic and anxiety disorders, insomnia and it stabilizes the blood pressure. As a result, it improves concentration, balances the nervous system and helps with emotional stability.

When I started practicing Yoga over 25 years ago, I was far from imagining all of the well-being, harmony and balance that it would bring into my life.

Every time I do Yoga, I only focus on emptying my inner self and on my breathing which helps me relax all of my muscles and nourish my body with Prana (vital energy).

During my Yoga practice, like magic, it seems that every question I have about my personal life, my family or my career suddenly has an answer. An answer to the "how," on what decision to make, on what is the perfect solution for a specific situation … it all seems to fall into place. Then, the ideas come by themselves and through inspiration, intuition and good guidance, Life fixes all things…

I love it!

▶ Yoga releases all of the stress, tension and cortisol (the stress hormone) that build up in the body because of the hectic life that we live nowadays.

▶ Yoga is an excellent complement to training or any other sport. It increases physical strength and endurance because it oxygenates every muscle of the body, a great addition for inveterate athletes!

WHERE CAN YOU DO YOGA?

In every city, small or big, there are excellent Yoga instructors to discover who can teach the basic asana techniques (positions) and pranayamas (breathing techniques).

I even think that there is a great ***Yoga/Tao Teacher** in the Laurentides region of Québec! Guess who? I know her very well! Spending a Wellness weekend of Yoga/Tao with her is truly the best! LOL! Ha ha ha! (*You can find her information in the **Bibliography** section of this book.)

In all of my Yoga/Tao Workshops/Classes, you can learn all of the breathing techniques (pranayamas) that I teach (6), they are very beneficial for the body. If you have the opportunity to learn these techniques from a certified teacher and to do them daily, your body and your mind will instantly feel rejuvenated.

What is truly amazing is that you can do Yoga anywhere… In a gym, in a Wellness Center, a Spa, on an all-inclusive vacation, in a Yoga class or at home!

So, everyone to your Yoga mats! Yoga is an actual "healthy lifestyle" that enhances your quality of life.

♥ 4 | Writing ♥

"WHAT WE EXPRESS IS NOT PRINTED OUT!"

Writing allows us to put on paper all the emotions that we are experiencing as if we were confiding to a close friend or a therapist. It is a very telling technique if we are able to be honest and "BE" ourselves.

As it is said, "What we express is not printed out!" So why wait, take a pen and paper and write down "**everything**" that you need to write to soothe your mind and empty the "overflows" that you have accumulated.

It is important to write everything that we are feeling, to write the bad feelings, the anger, sadness, sorrow, worry, stress, etc. **Use the first-person singular when you write**. First-person narration is the best way to have a great emotional release.

After, you can transform it with fire. (See section 5 for a complete description of the fire process.)

HOW TO STOP THE EMOTIONAL "BOILING POT" FROM OVERFLOWING ON THE PEOPLE WE LOVE?

You need to write "everything" that is weighing on your "Heart" to truly experience the "Heart Connection." This is where the miraculous power of the healing of the "Heart" comes from.

It is always better to write down everything that makes us suffer, to frcc our emotional overflow from unpleasant and hurtful situations that stem from rejection, abandonment, humiliation, injustice, betrayal, etc., instead of letting our pot "boil" with piled-up emotions (for too long) and that, unfortunately, "overflows" more often than not on the people we love.

Writing is a wonderful tool for us to evolve, to improve who we are as a person, to have the awareness of what is going on and change things accordingly in different areas of our lives.

When we write, there is no inhibition and we feel free of all judgement. The fear of expressing ourselves, of hurting the other or to disappoint the one we love goes away instantly because this process favors the healing of the "Heart" from one person to the other. Also … healing the "Heart" by writing is completely "magical!"

We only have to make the effort of writing what we are going through and transform it with fire, which solves our problem by 80% and even completely sometimes. So, of course, it is way more effective than dealing with a "magician"! … He can make an object disappear, but what about emotions? LOL!

Try this writing process… You will see extraordinary results as well as the beneficial and positive energies that this therapeutic process will bring in your life! It really is magical for our well-being!

♥ 5 | Fire ♥

PURIFICATION

Fire is very purifying. Looking at a candle, a fireplace or a campfire purifies the mind and the *"**Thought-Forms**" that are lacking light. The cleansing work is automatic, pleasant and does not require any effort. You just need to relax in a meditative or contemplative state or to laugh with friends by the fire.

This is why nights spent with friends around a campfire are often memorable. Fire also generates exceptional heat for the soul and the Heart.

This is why this song is very popular in Québec and known by all of the happy campers! … they all know it by heart! The song is called *"Feu, feu, joli feu"… which translates to "Fire, fire, pretty fire" in English.

If you feel a great lack of love, the heat of a cozy fireplace will undoubtedly fill you with a comforting feeling of well-being and a warm tenderness.

TRANSFORMING THE WRITINGS

Fire can also transform the written "overflows" into positive love energy for everyone who was mentioned in your writing. You just have to burn all of it in the fire, every page that you have written, and ask for them to be "transformed into love." Ask that everything be transformed in beneficial energy for your well-being and for the people around you, for the people that you see every day or for those who are mentioned in your writing.

Transforming our written emotions into love energy with fire is very therapeutic, even more so if we do not have the opportunity to express our feelings to a licensed therapist that can listen to us and help us empty our "overflows."

This technique is very effective and is the first technique that my mentor taught me 30 years ago when I was going through my first big transformation and "life transition." To write my emotions down on a piece of paper and burn them while asking for them to be transformed into "beneficial and positive energy" for myself and all those involved. This technique proves to still be useful each time an upsetting situation lingers in my mind and does not seem to get better, even after all the other cleansings that I do daily.

Once freed from my emotions, I am so happy that I start to sing the popular fire song **"Fire, fire, pretty fire…"** and my enthusiasm sometimes leads me to dance joyfully everywhere in my house!!! Absolutely everywhere!!! Lol!! … I make sure that I'm alone when I feel the need and the desire to celebrate arise! Lol!

*Song: *Fire, fire, pretty fire…

<u>Chorus</u>:

Fire, fire, pretty fire

Burning so bright

Fire, fire, pretty fire

All through the night

Through the night

<u>Verses</u>:

1– Long live the fire's heat, long live its heat!

2– Long live the fire's light, long live its light!

3– Long live the fire's splendor, long live its splendor!

4– Long live the fire's goodness, long live its goodness!

5– Long live the fire's colors, long live its colors!

6– Long live the fire's beauty, long live its beauty!

7– Long live the fire's labor, long live its labor!

8– Long live the fire's ember, long live its ember!

9– Long live the fire's smell, long live its smell!

10– Long live the fire's song, long live its song!

11– The flame is a gift from Heaven, long live the good Lord!

♥ 6 | Water ♥

WATER AND EMOTIONS

Water is linked to emotions. They can accumulate in the body, and drinking water helps us to deep clean and release our emotions. Water evacuates all the "overflows" of emotions. Drinking a large glass of water when we feel a sudden emotion helps us release it and come back to the Heart vibration.

Our body is made of 70% of water, hence why it is so important to hydrate ourselves regularly and to drink at least two liters of water every day. This natural cycle fills up the body with a renewed energy and naturally release the "overflows." It is like emptying a glass of water to fill it up again.

We empty the old one, the used water, we fill ourselves up with nice and clear water … and the deep cleaning happens during this process!

FASTING

That is the reason why taking the time to deep clean our body through "fasting" is very beneficial since water is the only neutralizing substance that we can usually consume during this deep cleaning period. Fasting is a natural practice that involves a food break that allows the body to take a break and results in the body's cell regeneration. The human body is amazing, it is able to regenerate itself. Fasting will clean it thoroughly.

Fasting has been known since the dawn of time and its therapeutic values have been known for centuries. Even in nature, animals are instinctively fasting when they are sick, hurt or hibernate. Numerous experiments on animal metabolism have shown that non-excessive restricted eating prolongs the lifespan of many species (mouse, rats, monkeys).

A study published in the ***Magazine *Nature*** in 2016 has also proven that fasting lowers damage done to the DNA.

Hippocrates recommended fasting to heal as well as prevent illnesses. Plato and Socrates have also praised the virtues of fasting. It is probably one of the most ancient approaches for self-healing known to date.

Why Fast?

Fasting purifies the entire organism, the body, the thoughts and every emotion. It is recommended to fast from time to time, at least once a year, or for one day occasionally. Fasting helps the body to rest and entirely cleans our meridians, liver, spleen, pancreas, intestines, kidneys, heart, lungs, etc., as well as all our "overflows."

Recommendations

It is recommended to fast under the supervision of a doctor or of a specialized center. It is also best to ask our doctor's opinion to make sure our health allows us to do it.

Types of Fasting

There are many types of fasting: the "daily fast" that lasts for a few hours, the "weekly fast" that is done one day a week, or the "full-wellness cure" that is done over a period of one week or more.

Since I do not have the time to fast completely and take ten consecutive days off for this full-wellness cure, I practice the "small fasts" ritual, called the "daily fast." It is beneficial for my system because it allows my body to rest for a few hours.

If my schedule allows it, two to three times a week, I fast in the morning until lunch time and, in the meantime, I drink "lemon water" in large quantities. The best "home remedy" I know of to clean the whole system!

THE TEN BENEFITS OF LEMON WATER

*(Reference: Dr. Alain Tuan Qui, Website: docteurbonnebouffe .com)

1 – Hydrates our Body:

Lemon has many important hydrating virtues since it is made with 80% water.

2 – Helps with Digestion:

Lemon water, when drunk on an empty stomach, eases the intestinal transit. Drinking lemon water "gets rid" of the wastes accumulated in the digestive mucosa and cleans the digestive system in order to better digestion. It also purifies the liver.

3 – Boost our Immune System:

Lemon is one of the foods that contains the most vitamin C: it helps us fight against temporary or chronic fatigue and is great for stimulating the immune system.

4 – Detoxifies the Body:

Lemon has detoxifying properties, it cleanses the digestive system.

It is also a mild and natural diuretic: it stimulates the kidneys, promoting the elimination of toxins from our body.

5 – Balances the Body's pH Level:

With its acidic taste, we tend to think that lemon would be acidifying. But it's not! Lemon, because of its citric acid content, mixes with minerals in the body and releases alkaline residues that have an anti-acidifying action. Because of its alkalizing action, lemon allows our body's pH to balance itself as soon as it is taken with water.

(*Reference: Book by Dr. Jacqueline Lagacé, "***Comment j'ai vaincu la douleur et l'inflammation chronique par l'alimentation***" [How I overcame pain and chronic inflammation through food.])

6 – Cleans the Skin:

In addition to all these detoxifying and diuretic properties, lemon added to lukewarm water helps to keep a healthy and glowing skin. Its alkaline nature destroys some of the bacteria that cause acne and other skin problems. The vitamin C and other antioxidants in lemon also help diminish wrinkles, blemishes and to fight free radicals, which are responsible for accelerated skin aging.

7 –A Natural Appetite Suppressant:

Lemon is an appetite suppressant because it contains pectin, a fiber that swells when in contact with water in the stomach. The lemon sends a message of satiety to prevent you from getting a little bit hungry or really hungry! Perfect for fasting!

8 – Makes You Lose Weight

Drinking lemon water in the morning on an empty stomach can also help you lose weight. In fact, as Dr. Alain Tuan Qui, a holistic health physician explains, "Lemon water helps you lose weight because when you improve your transit and improve your liver function, your body is optimized to burn fatty acids."

As a valuable thinning and detoxifying asset, lemon is also an excellent health food because it is rich in antioxidants that fight against free radicals that can damage cells! In short, lemon water is truly a miracle cure … use it as much as you like!

9 – How to Ingest Lemon Water?

The perfect ratio of lemon water, in order to maximize its benefits for our body, is a quarter of a lemon for a glass of water. It is important to make sure that the water is lukewarm (room temperature), not too hot, not too cold. The ideal temperature for lemon water is that of our body, which is 37 °C.

Another important point: the origin of the lemon. Always use fresh lemons, preferably organic (to avoid pesticides in your health drink!) Drink a glass of this preparation on an empty stomach, 15 to 20 minutes before breakfast or during a fast. There is nothing better than this healthy drink to start your day!

10 – Recommendations:

Lemon juice is not recommended, especially on an empty stomach, **in cases of ulcers, gastritis or esophageal reflux** because of its natural acidity. It is also not recommended for **"neuro-arthritic"** people, who risk acidification with lemon. Also, do not forget that the acidity of lemon **can weaken our dental enamel**. The website docteurbonnebouffe.com recommends drinking lemon water through a straw, for example, and to **never brush your teeth immediately after drinking lemon water.**

BALNEOTHERAPY AND ITS FIVE BENEFITS

Taking therapeutic baths helps to liberate the tensions and the "overflows" of life. In addition to providing exceptional relaxation for the mind, body and spirit!

The **term balneotherapy** comes from the Latin *balneum*, which means "bath".

Balneotherapy is considered to be one of the most powerful natural therapeutic agents, which provides surprising health benefits. It is very easy to experiment, it is a treatment that uses running water in a bathtub to which you can add marine products such as seaweed, sea salt or sea mud, essential oils, therapeutic flowers, etc.

You can do balneotherapy in a whirlpool bath or simply in a nice warm bath.

I can say that I have been loving Balneotherapy for a very long time and that it provides me with exceptional benefits in my daily life. After a hard day at work, it's the perfect way to relieve myself of all the stresses and strains of the day. I started this practice after I simply needed to relax after a hard day's work, but over the years I have developed a regular habit of alternating between mud, seaweed, sea salt and essential oil baths.

Taking a bath or a shower in the awareness that we are cleansing our *"**Energetic Bodies**" helps cleanse the *"**Auric Body**" and the *"**Emotional Body**". The more aware we are, the more cleansing is done and we feel relaxed. A sea salt bath is recommended for this kind of cleansing.

1 – The Properties of Balneotherapy

The therapeutic proprieties of Balneotherapy are found in seawater, seaweed, sea salts and marine or ground mud. These elements are very rich in minerals, vitamins and trace elements (iodine, calcium, phosphorus). All of these therapeutic elements from the sea (and from the earth; the ground mud) nourish and oxygenate the cells.

Balneotherapy has multiple benefits.

It helps with muscle tone, digestion, healthy eating and promotes the elimination of dead cells and toxins from the body. By stimulating blood circulation, it relieves internal congestion and delays the development of varicose veins. It also has beneficial effects on the cardiovascular system. It also eliminates calcium deposits in the blood vessels.

2 – A Balneotherapy Cure

A Balneotherapy cure is the perfect way to release accumulated stress. It is beneficial to the whole body. Put it in your agenda, as you do for your family vacations. Except that this vacation is, in fact, just for you. Plan a whole week, or 3 to 4 days, depending on your needs and your schedule, even a few hours will help your well-being!

Each year, when the moment for my Balneotherapy Cure comes, I am so happy, it is like a great gift "from me, to me, because I love myself!" It is a moment when I find myself again, when I only think about me and I let go of everything that does not serve me! These encounters with myself are necessary in order to maintain balance in my life and my happiness, so I try to put them in my daily schedule or I do small Balneotherapy cures one or twice a year. When I had my own Spa/Wellness Center for 18 years, I planned a four-day-intensive care twice a year, in the spring and in the fall. Sometimes, I went to other Spas and Wellness Balneotherapy Centers for cures that lasted from a week to ten days. Now, I have everything I need at home, so I do these types of cures as often as possible … especially when I realize that the whirlwind of life has taken a toll on my schedule, my *joie de vivre* and my quality of life!

3 – Hot Tubs

Hot tubs help cure the cold and the flu, they are ideal for winter. Inhaling water vapor helps to cure the cold and the flu and is highly recommended if you have a sinus infection, bronchitis, allergies or asthma. One Balneotherapy session that lasts 15 to 20 minutes, with a mix of sea salt and good essential oils, like eucalyptus or pine, is enough to retrieve all the benefits. The baths should be taken three times a week for optimal results.

You can find therapeutic products to add to your bath like algae, mud, mixes of sea salts and essential oils in health and wellness stores, or in any good Spa/Wellness Centre that will help you find the best products according to your needs.

4 – Hydromassages

Hydromassages have a calming effect on the nervous system and relax the muscles. The water jets tone the body and reinvigorate sore muscles. They also help with the sensation of heavy legs as well as back, neck and foot pain and it drains the lymphatic system because of the powerful jets.

5 – Balneotherapy Clears the Skin

Balneotherapy deep cleans the skin, improves the skin's elasticity, makes it firmer … and refines the silhouette.

It is perfect to stay beautiful, young and healthy! After a Balneotherapy session, we truly feel regenerated and freed from our "overflows" … that's for sure!

As Jacques-Yves Cousteau, a French ocean explorer, once said, "We are born from water, it is in water that appeared the first living cells. Water and our lives are tied together."

Nowadays, technology allows us to enjoy the benefits of Balneotherapy at home … so, let us enjoy it! Now is the time to make yourself a nice relaxing bath!

MY PERSONAL AT HOME "OPTIMAL CURE" FOR COMPLETE RELAXATION

It is my personal optimal cure for a full relaxation… After a long week of work, it is important for me to start my weekend by sleeping in, relaxing and spending at least five to six hours doing what I call **"settling."** By that I mean putting the daily life that sometimes goes too fast on pause. Rest, relax and move a little, get some fresh air and/or exercise. I personally choose a sport that I like, because it usually helps me relax and get rid of the "overflows" in my mind. I like to continue to relax by taking a bath or getting in a sauna and, afterwards, I get a Neuromassage on the therapeutic chair. At that point, believe me, I am completely relaxed and sleeping soundly… The whole shebang!

It is almost like a day at the Spa, it gives me guaranteed relaxation in order to really unwind from my week, "settle" and empty all of my "overflows"… Of course, everyone has their own way of "settling"…

WATER AND THE SEA

The therapeutic virtues of the sea are very beneficial for us. Sitting by the sea is purifying, because salt air purifies our *"**Aura**". Also, a good swim in the sea cleanses our emotional body because of the salt water. It is not surprising that so many people want to go to tropical and seaside places!

Getting away from it all with a seaside vacation allows us to come back completely recharged and rejuvenated, even if most of the time we are not even aware of it! So, taking long walks on the beach and swimming in the sea multiple times a day is indisputably a great wellness cure!

And what's more, it is a great reason to book a trip to a tropical destination and telling your partner, "Honeeeeyyyy, would you like to go empty your 'overflows' somewhere nice and hot?" and they answer, "My over-what?" Lol!

♥ 7 | Internal Health Cures ♥

Enjoying **Health Cures** to cleanse the body a few times a year has a lot of benefits and helps get rid of the "overflows." By ridding the body of its waste and impurities, we get rid of everything that does not serve us and that we do not need in our life in order to move forward. We get rid of the built-up toxins and the "overflows" of our lives at the same time. As one might say, getting rid of the old!

THE BEST TIME OF THE YEAR TO DO A "WELLNESS CURE" AND TO START FRESH!

Spring and fall are the best to start fresh and deep clean our houses, our wardrobes and our body. For example, in spring we clean our backyards that have accumulated the dirt of winter and prepare our gardens and our flower beds for summer, and fall is perfect for a cleanup after our vacations and before the back-to-school season.

It is the same thing for our body. In the spring, we can deep clean ourselves to free ourselves from what we have accumulated during winter. And in the fall, we can let go of the excesses of the summer time that has built up in our bodies.

Getting rid of what does not serve us anymore and of all our "overflows" is very good. It is as important to do this for our body as it is important to change the oil in a car!

During spring and fall, it is time to do a little cleansing by doing an "internal Wellness Cure." We can find it in specialized shops, like a good health food store, where you can ask for a professional's help.

Doing a "Wellness Cure" helps free ourselves from toxins and stress (cortisol) and gives a full cleanse of all of our meridians and our internal organs (liver, spleen, pancreas, kidneys, lungs, heart, intestines).

How to Get the Best Results During your "Wellness Cure"?

In order to have the best results during your "Wellness Cure," try at the same time to get back into shape by practicing physical activity, to enjoy nature, to do a lot of outside activities and to practice yoga. Without forgetting to give yourself a "small spring time or fall time gift" by enjoying hot tubs, saunas or getting a nice massage … it is up to you!

Taking time for yourself is important, it will help your body to free itself from the energetic and muscular tensions as well as all the stress it accumulates daily. Physical, emotional and mental wellness guaranteed!

It is recommended to do this type of "Wellness Cure" once or twice a year, in the spring time and the fall time. Doing an occasional "Wellness Cure" brings back our vitality, the body rejuvenation that we are looking for after the winter months or an overbooked summer and gives us the necessary boost to start our new projects and be in good health!

Yes! Let's go! Find the perfect time for a nice "Wellness Cure"! Your body will thank you! The results will surprise you, because it will be a good cleanse of the body as well as the soul and the mind!

♥ 8 | Tao ♥

The **TAO** techniques are useful to purify the "overflows" by cleansing our energetic bodies.

Tao exercises, done smoothly and gently, are very efficient techniques to empty the "overflows" of heavy energies accumulated in our aura.

It is important to know that before entering our "physical body," the "overflows" that often become illnesses first enter our "astral bodies" *(Aura).

So, releasing the overflows regularly using Tao prevents us from accumulating physical, moral, mental and emotional pain.

ENERGY TAO AND OPENING OF THE HEART

Energy Tao is a mix between simple and easy-to-learn techniques to help with stress, calm the mind, ease anxiety and daily tensions, boost the immune system, make a big energetic cleanse and purify the *"Subtle Bodies": *"Mental," *"Emotional," and *"Celestial Body".

You can practice Tao standing, sitting or lying on the floor, it is subtle and soft, and the relaxing motions raise vital energy. Practicing it regularly brings new vitality and helps us to keep our health.

The Tao techniques stimulate the *joie de vivre*, give us peace of mind and help it rest.

The thoughts become calmer, more peaceful, which helps us make better decisions. So, we become more efficient and enthusiastic in our life every day.

Diligently practicing Tao allows the "**Heart opening**." A feeling of uniqueness, profoundness and inner quietness comes from it. Integrating these Tao techniques connects us not only to our Heart, but also to the reality of life, allowing us to appreciate its power and its beauty.

When our "subtle bodies" are aligned, "listening to our Heart" becomes way easier. Without any effort, the "Heart Connection" can unfold naturally and shine on its own.

I have been practicing these Tao techniques for more than 25 years. It is in Guadeloupe, after finishing all my training, that I began to teach them. Since then I cannot go one morning without at least 10 minutes of these "energizing techniques" that actually bring happiness at the beginning of each day!

Doing these Tao techniques for 10 to 15 minutes after waking up is like saying hello to Life and opening up to everything it has to offer for the day ahead!

♥ 9 | Massages ♥

Massages ... a True "Youth Cure!"

Who doesn't need to escape a little, far away from it all, in order to recharge your batteries and receive a great **MASSAGE** to release our "overflows" of life? Yes! Massages are exceptionally effective to free us from tensions because a lot of our "overflows" are stuck in our nerve endings and in our muscles.

Everyone should allow themselves to "take time out," enjoy a relaxing break and appreciate the benefits of a great massage because it also gives us a "long-life elixir."

Massage is a true "Youth Cure" for the mind, the body and the soul. It allows us to free ourselves from physical, emotional and mental tensions … which also helps with slowing down the "aging process."

It really is a "Youth Cure" just like in a "Fountain of Youth" or a "Fountain of Life."

A process that helps to regenerate all of our cells, soothes our aches, promotes a resting period, allows us to find balance and inner harmony and it keeps us healthy.

ONE OF THE MOST ANCIENT THERAPEUTIC METHODS

Since the dawn of time, massage therapy helps to heal and release all kinds of aches. It probably is one of the oldest treatments for pain. It is one of the forms of popular therapy that has been developed and adapted, in ancient times, by people from all continents. Ancients called it "touch therapy," it was practiced by the laying on of hands and with other kinds of techniques, each one more unique than the other. Among the Persians, massage was done with the hands and the feet. Massages have always been an instinctive practice.

The multiple virtues of massage therapy and the enthusiasm for this type of relaxation are no stranger to today's stressful way of living where everything must always go faster and where performance is of uncompromising rigor. Taking time to breathe, slowing down from the crazy pace of life, calm the mind, reset, all of it is essential for good health.

As the Roman saying goes: "healthy mind in a healthy body"… Which means that "having a healthy body" will inevitably help us to have a "healthy mind" and vice versa!

DIFFERENT TYPES AND TECHNIQUES OF MASSAGES

We are lucky, because nowadays there are a lot of different types and techniques of massages available. Wellness Centers specialize in massages: relaxation massage, sports massage, therapeutic massage, four-hand massage, massage for pregnant women and children, hot stone massage, lymphatic drainage massage, reflexology massage, laying on of hands massage, etc. Each technique is adapted to what the person wants and what they are looking for.

The Swedish massage is undoubtedly the most popular, the most traditional and the most practiced technique in the Western World. We owe this massage technique to an avant-garde Swedish man named Pehr Henrick Ling who wanted to share his knowledge for the greater good.

The Swedish massage reduces stress, helps with eliminating nervous tension, promotes better blood circulation and lymphatic circulation, eliminates accumulated toxins and relaxes the muscles. Its recognized maneuvers, such as gentle or deep effleurage, kneading, percussion, friction, joint work, drainage, etc., make it the dream massage for many.

Some will choose to buy a massage chair (or massage cushion for chairs) or even a sophisticated machine. But nothing replaces human hands and an excellent massage given by a great massage therapist in a Wellness Centre where the atmosphere, the intimacy and the customer service are developed and organized according to the well-being of the client. Finally, you can appreciate and recognize the work, the generosity and the selflessness of a professional massage therapist who gives their services with love and attention.

So, paying for a good massage is the perfect occasion to take care of yourself and to have an occasional treat. The frequency and consistency of a massage have unexpected benefits on the body and the mind, it cleanses our body of our "overflows" without us even noticing! It really is the very best!

After a good treatment, we truly feel free of our resistance and our worries while feeling lighter, as if the weight of life had disappeared! Try it, you will be surprised to see how relaxed and rejuvenated you will feel. Receiving a great massage by a specialized, certified and professional massage therapist is pure happiness. You will feel a kind of renewed youth, worthy of a "Youth Cure"!

Having been the owner of a Balneotherapy and Massage Therapy Spa for many years (18 years), I was lucky enough to be spoiled once every two weeks! There were so many benefits and I felt rejuvenated each time. In my Spa, the room where I preferred to receive my spa treatments was called "Cleopatra"… However, that does not mean that I became the beautiful "Cleopatra"! Lol! A girl can dream … right?

Happy massage!

♥ 10 | Saunas ♥

THE FINNISH SAUNA

The Sauna is a social tradition that has existed for over 2,000 years in Nordic countries. It is a health ritual that originated in Finland. As its name suggests, the "Finlandia" sauna is in the purest tradition of the Nordic sauna. It is set up in a spacious building made of solid wood, in a small wooden hut or in a room where you take a "dry heat" bath, which can vary from 70 °C to 100 °C and is very beneficial for your well-being. Taking a sauna consists of staying in a room heated to a high temperature for a few moments, then leaving it to enjoy the variation between the hot and the cold. The effect of the heat and the cold of this ritual make it particularly good for the skin's balance and for our health.

WHAT THE SAUNA DOES TO THE BODY

When entering the "dry sauna," the body is confronted with a temperature of around 80 °C, depending on the type of sauna and the power of the heater.

▶ The reaction of the cardiovascular system to this temperature is immediate: dilation of the blood vessels and an increased heart rate;

▶ The skin begins to sweat profusely, the pores dilate.

▶ The body releases endorphins, which helps to relax.

▶ After 10 to 15 minutes, you leave the sauna to take a cold shower or a bath. The cold action tightens the pores and revitalizes the body.

▶ Afterwards, it is wise to take time to rest and relax for 20 minutes outside the sauna, between each hot and cold cycle.

▶ You then repeat the hot and cold cycles up to three times. Rehydrate yourself by drinking water between each sauna session in order to recover the water you sweated. It is indeed possible to lose up to one liter of water during a sauna session.

THE 6 BENEFITS OF THE SAUNA

The heat of the sauna and the various hot and cold cycles have significant benefits for the body.

1 – The Relaxing Aspect of the Sauna:

A sauna session is very effective to reduce stress, tension and all the fatigue accumulated because of our "overflows." Because of the heat, the body releases endorphins that promote relaxation and sleep. When used just before going to bed, the sauna helps you sleep better.

2 – The Purifying Aspect of the Sauna:

The dry heat of the sauna causes a lot of sweating and opens up the pores. Sweating helps to get rid of the toxins accumulated in the body. A good sauna session results in the purification of the body and the mind.

3 – The Muscular and Cardiovascular Aspect of the Sauna:

By dilating the blood vessels, the sauna helps the cardiovascular system to function properly. It also helps to keep blood pressure low. Finally, the increase of blood circulation while you are in the sauna helps to quickly relieve muscle pain and other aches. A new study published by the medical journal *JAMA Internal Medicine* states that women and men who regularly attend saunas seem to reduce their risk of death caused by a cardiovascular disease and even mortality of any cause. Sauna sessions are therefore recommended to maintain good health! The Finns have understood that for a long time!

4 – The Benefits of the Sauna for the Finns:

Throughout history, the Finns and saunas were always one. For centuries, from their youngest age, the Finns have been initiated to this practice. Sauna is a way of life, and it remains with them throughout their lives.

In winter, the often-freezing temperatures offer a contrast between hot and cold that is highly appreciated by enthusiasts who are delighted to alternate between pleasure and thrill. Diving into the icy water of the lakes and rolling around in the snow is said to be good for blood circulation, even if most Finns do it mainly for the incredible boost it gives them.

The Finnish adjective "Saunanjälkeinen" is used to describe the unique state of serenity one experiences when leaving the sauna, this "soothing" state after a sauna is considered in our country to be a valid excuse for doing nothing, since everyone is free to indulge in this beneficial emptiness state for as long as they like.

5 – Boosting the Immune System with the Sauna:

The sauna makes the body sweat which stimulates the immune system and increases the production of white blood cells and antibodies in order to fight diseases. Having regular sauna sessions could even protect us from flu epidemics.

6 – Saunas Benefit the Skin

By opening up the pores, using a sauna helps the skin to release toxins. It also softens the skin and improves its elasticity.

The cold shower (or cold bath) that one must take after the sauna then tightens the pores and improve the appearance of the skin.

SAUNA: COMPARING TYPES OF SAUNAS

(See pictures in the Glossary)

There are different types of saunas to choose from depending on the energy used.

There is the *"**Traditional Sauna**" with wood or gas, the *"**Sauna with an electric heater**" and the *"**Infrared Sauna**". I recommend the latter, it is the one I use at home because I do not have to always feed the wood stove of the traditional sauna or to water the volcanic stones of the electric stove.

The temperature rises quickly in the infrared sauna and is less suffocating than the traditional sauna where the intense heat raises the ambient temperature and makes it difficult to breathe since the air becomes too dry. In the infrared sauna, however, the heat is directed into the body instead of raising and heating the temperature inside the sauna.

The important thing during a session is to feel comfortable with the temperature and to stay for at least 10 to 15 minutes or until you see water droplets all over your body. But be careful! When you feel like you are literally melting, it's a sign that it's time to go! LOL!

Try it and you'll love it! I could not live without it because I love the feeling it gives me.

After several years of visiting Nordic Spas, I finally decided to have one at home. It is a profitable investment because I use it all year long. I jump in the lake until it freezes over in December and then start again in the spring as soon as the ice starts to melt. During the colder winter months, the snow provides the hot and cold contrast necessary for this very beneficial health ritual.

When you are rolling around in the snow, do not be afraid to become an actual "snowman," your body heat will melt the snow in no time! LOL!

♥ 11 | Exercise ♥

EXERCISE AND "HAPPY HORMONES"

Exercise is an efficient remedy to cleanse any kind of heaviness in our body, it moves our energy and stimulates the production of endorphins, also called "happy hormones."

***Endorphins** are hormones released by the brain as soon as we exercise for longer than 30 minutes. They are a source of wellness if they are released in large quantities because they can induce a euphoric or ecstatic state.

What people like from these natural hormones is the feeling of euphoria that occurs as soon as our brain releases them.

The "endorphins" have many benefits for the body. They reduce our stress levels, have rejuvenating and anti-fatigue properties, and they create a sensation of relaxation and wellness that make us happy.

Those endorphins give us a feeling of "Happiness." In fact, our brain releases them when we do physical activity and when it feels "Happy!"

So, imagine that you are training while feeling happy, your happiness will be multiplied since "Happiness creates Happiness!"

INCREASED LEVELS OF SEROTONIN AND DEPRESSION

Both *"**Endorphins**" and *"**Serotonin**," a necessary molecule to our *joie de vivre*, have an antidepressant effect.

It has been scientifically proven that "serotonin" plays an important role in our "mood swings" and that it greatly influences our daily emotional state. A "serotonin imbalance" can provoke an "anxious state."

Regular physical activity increases serotonin in the brain and reduces symptoms of depression. Among other things, depression decreases the level of serotonin in the body. Even if several brain-related causes are linked to depression, such as hormones, neurotransmitters combined with social, psychological and even genetic factors, it has been said that exercising regularly increases the natural release of serotonin, helps us regulate the symptoms of depression and helps us get our good mood back!

RESPECTING YOUR LIMITS

It can be very hard to start exercising, even more so if you have a lot of "overflows" like after a big disappointment, a major life transition, a career change, a separation, grieving or trying to get better after an illness. It is better to start with other release techniques, all very gentle, as we have seen in the previous chapters. Later on, once our "overflows" have been released in different ways or by doing gentle physical exercise, we will be able to return to a more intense physical practice to regularly empty our "overflows."

The important thing is to listen to yourself, because if we force things and push our resistance when we have too much built up, we fill our tank of "overflows" instead of emptying it. Since it will take too much of an effort to get there, we give up right away without reaching our goal.

It is better, at the beginning, to practice soft sports, the ones that do not require much effort. When the time comes, you will be able to get back to exercising and do the sport of your choice that brings you both joy and a feeling of wellness.

When there is too much accumulation, making an effort and having discipline to train also becomes an "overflow" from which we must free ourselves. We can therefore start exercising with gentler activities such as walking, yoga, tai chi, Tao and then progress at our own pace without forcing ourselves to perform or force things. And like magic, our "Happiness Hormones" are there!

So, gradually, regular physical exercise will come to us effortlessly with joy and happiness in our heart!

15 Minutes of Exercise Each Day

Did you know that only 15 minutes of exercise each day can extend the life expectancy by three years on average? Doing 15 minutes of exercise each day is nothing in a 24-hour day! All it takes is some willpower and some decisiveness! It is often the most difficult part, even more difficult than the exercise itself. But when we do it, we feel a great satisfaction.

So, find the exercise you like best, the easiest, the one that does not ask too much of you to start, the one you love the most, and do it for 15 minutes! Health and longevity guaranteed!

And if one day, all of a sudden, you see me passing by your house running, follow me! It is way easier to do it with another person, you can motivate each other and it really helps! LOL!

♥ 12 | Food ♥

Food and Guilt

The "overflows" often come from **food**, because we often feel "guilty" to have eaten something that comforts us and makes us feel good.

By emptying our emotional "overflows," we do not eat our emotions as much and it makes the culpability tank of "overflows" smaller. Talk about a win-win!

To do so, we must look at ourselves and realize that if we eat, and sometimes eat too much, because of our emotions and because of culpability, it is because we are compensating for something else. We must look inside, what "overflow" am I eating right now? … Stress, anxiety, worry, sadness, anger, fear, emotional dependency, etc.? It is like a never-ending vicious cycle, each time we eat our emotions, we feel guilty. So, these emotions and this guilt builds up and it needs to be dealt with first.

By taking care of things when they first come up, the rest falls into place. So, we eliminate the guilt we feel each time we "let" ourselves have a comforting treat.

Guilt is a result of a "lack" of many different things and it unfortunately gnaws at us from the inside. We must solve this problem and balance these destructive behaviors in order to enjoy what Life has to offer. If we do not do it, it is impossible to let go and enjoy our life fully and freely.

Food, in addition to being essential to a good health, is one of the simple pleasures of life. "To be an epicurean" is to love the good life and look for the simple and great pleasures Life can give. We need to enjoy it a little! The trick is to do it in a balanced way, so we can be filled with happiness!

♥ 13 | Silence ♥

SILENT RETREAT

Sometimes, going to a **Silent** retreat or allowing ourselves small intervals of silence in the day can be very beneficial for our mental and emotional state.

Gifting ourselves a 10-day silent retreat from time to time like in an Ashram or in a specialized center allows us to truly touch this unique zone of mystical peace of the soul deeply inside us. One we have touched this zone and contacted our inner source, which is a "heavenly manna" of advice and divine directions, it inevitably brings us back to it from time to time.

It then becomes a necessity, which we find more and more important in our daily life because the sensation brings us such a good feeling of wellness.

LISTEN TO THE "VOICE OF SILENCE"

The easiest way to listen to the "voice of silence" is by being in contact with the greatness of nature.

Contemplating and observing nature releases a lot of stress.

It allows us to empty all of our "overflows" and completely rejuvenate ourselves when we reconnect with its great power, which truly is a source of advice and direction in our life. It is up to us to decide if we want to take a small vacation in silence in it! Or even take a few hours of our time to take a nice stroll in the forest.

Occasionally, I love to go to the yoga Ashram for a 10-day silent retreat. Yes! Ten days of silence to empty my mind, meditate, do yoga and not talk. It really is an exceptional experience. Our mind becomes clear and limpid and our intuition increases tenfold, what a unique sensation! It is a gift to offer ourselves at least once in a lifetime.

This kind of silent retreat allows me to put my brain in neutral for several days, to completely calm my mind and to experience a feeling of inner peace that cannot be described.

When I am back home, it sometimes takes me three to four days before I really feel like talking again, still being in this state of salutary bliss…

The only problem is that my husband is concerned that I lost my voice during my stay! LOL! But when everything is back to normal, I can tell you that I am making up for the lost time … and that I am telling in detail all the magnificent moments and encounters spent in the company of the *"**Great Masters**" Yogis of the Ashram.

♥ 14 | Order ♥

PUTTING THINGS IN ORDER

Putting things in **Order** daily is really important because with order comes a clear mind.

The more we cleanse our emotions, our thoughts and even our old beliefs or our outdated behaviors, the more we are able to live a centered and peaceful life guided by intuition.

Cleaning up your life and cleansing things thoroughly requires courage and often scares people. A lot of us are afraid of the disturbances it creates and fear that they will have to face the emotions that are brought to the surface. Shaking up our old emotions that we have not dealt with is not always easy, but we must face them and take our time; otherwise Life will do it for us… I can guarantee you! It will create circumstances that force us to relive certain unpleasant situations in order for us to settle them, cleanse them and change them for the better.

GETTING OUR THOUGHTS AND EMOTIONS IN ORDER

Whether it is taking the time to set something straight with an acquaintance, a family member, a partner, a friend, a colleague, a boss or to settle a situation in which we are in for no reason, it is all the same.

We need to put our thoughts and our emotions in order and do things to free ourselves from this inner mess, this "overflow" that this situation is causing. It is very important that we take the necessary steps to achieve a feeling of emotional balance and inner peace.

If we do not fix anything, even when we feel like we should, because the circumstances are too hard to bear, the situation will get worse every day and get to a point where it will explode. Our emotions will grow until they reach a level of intense anger, resentment and hate. This is not great but we all go through it one day or another.

As we go through different life experiences, we learn to settle things quickly. We also learn to respect our limits, to clean and cleanse our life as soon as we feel that a situation, a meeting, a discussion or different important life circumstances are detrimental or make us "thrown a fit!" No … but really, it's not only the kids that can do it! LOL.

To find the order in all that, we need to look at what we are truly feeling about this situation: **rejection**, **betrayal**, **abandonment**, **injustice** or **humiliation**. These principal characteristics are linked to old inner wounds that we need to heal in order to stop reopening them over and over. All of the physical, emotional or mental problems come from these five important wounds.

I strongly recommend reading the number one book sold in the French-speaking world and best-seller with more than two million copies sold: *"**Heal Your Wounds and Find Your True Self**"*, written by my friend and internationally successful author Lise Bourbeau. The techniques that she teaches in her book will allow you to identify these wounds and give you the necessary tools to heal them.

Cleaning and Tidying Up

Strangely, getting things in order for our inner self while putting things in order physically, aka cleaning, helps us see certain situations with more clarity.

This means that cleaning our houses, wardrobes, office, papers, our sheds, our cars, our backyards, etc. helps us have a clear and functioning state of mind which helps us move forward.

It means that finally, cleaning helps us let go of our possessions, facilitates a necessary detachment regarding what is no longer useful and, at the same time, frees us from all the "overflows" of our life. YES!!!!!!! Cleaning, however you want, helps solve many situations in life and helps us see clearly what we have to do next!

ORDER and CLEANLINESS = CLEAR MINDSET
"INNER and PHYSICAL" ORDER brings DIVINE ORDER into our lives.

So, get your brooms out! … To live happy, healthy and with a clear mindset!

Chapter 12

The Mental, Emotional and Physical Relief

♥ 1 | The Goal is to Evacuate All of our "Overflows" ♥

We are here on this Earth to relieve our body from matter, even if we live in a terrestrial body, we must relieve our suffering, our resistance, our fears, our stress. We already talked about it a lot, but it is essential to develop tools and techniques to learn how to free ourselves from what makes our body, our soul and our mind heavier.

This is why taking the time to "release things every day" is our number one goal.

♥ 2 | Relief Guides us Toward the "Heart Connection" ♥

Feeling relief inevitably guides us toward our true essential needs and directly to the "Heart Connection" in order for us to connect with our intuition as often as possible. So, the more time we take on the terrestrial plane each day to "release" worries, anxieties, fears, etc., the more we are in contact with the Light that shines within our Heart, which is in fact the most faithful guide you will ever get in your life!

It is also there that we can feel the biggest comforting feeling of our life. It is there that we start feeling loved by Life, supported by Life, confident with Life, since it loves us like a "mother caring for her child." And if we give ourselves the necessary time to release ourselves every day, we can "BE" in contact with this great power of Life and peacefully let ourselves be guided by it.

But when the whirlwind of emotions is present and the fear gets stronger and the distress takes over, we often feel powerless, submerged by all these emotions and incapable to connect to the power of the Heart.

This prevents us from feeling the strength of Life. The tip to get there is to dive head first into these feelings, to accept them, to feel the sorrow, the deception and the sadness they bring. It is only when we have "accepted," "welcomed" and "purified" them that we can achieve the "Heart Connection."

The more we enter the "Light of the Heart," the more we will want to come back because it is where we learn to "BE" at peace and aligned with our soul's needs. The objective is to be able to evacuate all the "overflows" of our life.

You can achieve this by practicing:

▶ **"mental releases," by meditating;**

▶ **"emotional releases," by expressing your emotions and accepting to feel them;**

► to "release your physical body" from the stress of daily life by exercising, practicing physical activity or any kind of gentle technique like yoga, etc.

So, if by "releasing" you are starting to hear "the sound of silence" it is because you are on the right path. Carry on… And if one day you feel an all-around sense of relief and that you are more and more relieved … as light as a feather! … and that all of a sudden, you feel like you are seeing Angels … it probably is because you are levitating! LOL! Which means that you have now perfectly followed your path on Earth and that you might be in Heaven, and it is now your turn to help others! LOL! … Or you are already a devoted and generous "Terrestrial Angel," as we often see these days!

Enough joking, these moments of grace that we touch with the "Heart Connection" are those that allow us to carry on with life, to be fulfilled, to attract what we want most and to truly "BE" happy.

♥ 3 | The "Heart Connection" and the Law of Attraction ♥

This is when the Law of Attraction truly activates. The more we are in contact with this sensation of wellness, the more we radiate the true essence of our Heart and Soul, which automatically attracts what we truly desire. In other words, to "BE" in synergy with our Heart's truth. Connecting every day to our Heart's essence allows the glow of our "BEING" to shine brighter, the magnitude of the love we carry within us.

Then, our path becomes easier to follow, because the obstacles of the "overflows" are released to leave space for the "guidance of the Heart."

This connection allows us to generate unconditional love so it can be manifested without any effort. We then become aware that the judgements, doubts, disappointments and worries that we had are slowly fading away. As I mentioned before, it is then that the famous phrase makes the most sense: **"The entire Universe conspires for my happiness and puts everything into place for me to be happy!"**

It is simple, we must be able to get into this zone that brings us so much guidance, infinite resources, knowledge and great joy in life. Because it is there that we find "Heaven on Earth," in the "Heart Connection" zone, inside us, even if we are going through a rough patch and big life transitions. Remember LIFE's answer in Chapter 4:

"Even in suffering, darkness and shadow, there is light. In those tough times, you need to stop and look within you to find the light. It is the light of the 'Heart Connection' that transforms everything with its radiation."

When we are able to get into it regularly, it is like a reunion each time, we want to come back to it as often as possible! So, we develop all kinds of ways to insert the "Heart Connection" into our life to benefit from the positive forces of life. *"MERCI LA VIE !"* for the greatness of your Love!

I can now confirm that this **"life transition,"** this **"forced transition"** that Life has imposed on me was in fact a formidable GIFT to me: writing this book filled with gentleness of the Heart and amazing tools to live a better life. Despite the hard times, filled with difficult and painful moments (like I have often felt during this process), these experiences have helped me grow on so many levels…

Now, I must be at least six-foot-one (6'-1" – 1.85 meters). YES! Yes! I am taller and taller … (on the inside!) So, you're telling me that I can finally reach the top shelf!!? LOL!

♥ 4 | The "Heart Connection" and Interpersonal Relationships ♥

The Heart Connection truly favors great connections in our relationships. Nonetheless, if you sometimes feel that there is some hiccups in your relationship with certain people, this is a strong indication that there is a lack of chemistry or kinship in the relationship. It can also just be because the "Heart Connection" will not work because of all of these barriers that we have talked about in previous chapters.

Sometimes, it can be a one-way "Heart Connection," meaning that you are in your Heart, but not the others. This principle also applies the other way around, meaning that the others are in their Heart, but not you. So, when these moments come, it is time to take a moment of introspection and come back home!

If the relationship is complicated, or even impossible, it is because the other person has blockages. But do not be scared, sooner or later if you truly stay connected to your Heart, the vibration will get to the other person or persons. This is the power of Love!

– "The positive forces" are always stronger than the negative ones.

– "The Light" always has the last word even when facing darkness, negativity or blockages in our lives.

**Yes! "The Light and the positive forces"
that "Love" represents are always stronger
than darkness, negative energy and the
walls put up by the ego.**

It is up to us to get what we truly want! We must persevere and always come back to this "Heart Connection."

<u>Example of everyday life:</u>

When there is a conflict between two people, instead of thinking "They did this to me, they are like that, it is because of them that, etc.," think of all the negative aspects of this relationship and then concentrate on the "Heart Connection." This helps make the situation the way you want it to be. Take what does not suit you and transform it into positive energy with sentences that express how you want to feel.

"I love being in harmony with ____________."

"I love to be respected by ______________."

"I love to be loved by ___________________."

"I love to be surrounded by nice, open-minded people whose hearts are filled with goodness."

Etc.

Try it! You'll see, it works every time!

Because the "energy of the Heart" always gets to the right person and/or brings amazing change in different situations!

♥ 5 | The "Heart Connection" and Returning to our Roots ♥

"BEING" in the "Heart Connection" is like coming home, returning to our roots, to the essence of who we truly are. The "Heart Connection" also allows us to connect with our own truth. It gets rid of all the false beliefs and illusions of our life that are not aligned, most of the time, with what we truly want or who we truly are.

The more we "let go" of the control we want to have on our life, the easier it is to make the "Heart Connection" from our head to our Heart!

Of course, the more we are into the "Heart Connection," the more we meet people who also are in the "Heart Connection." Resulting in a lot of Heart-to-Hearts and deep relationships! Without any judgement, obstacles or egocentric exchanges.

The "Heart Connection" is the awakening that we all want to have in our lives.

And the good news is that we can truly experience it every day if we really want to! This reality is accessible to whoever wants to!

We only need to choose to live our life according to the "Heart Connection!"

My dear friends, this is what I wish for everyone. Imagine all the happy encounters to come if we all lived in harmony and in "Connection with our Heart"… Party time! This could even have a great impact on world peace and between all people of the Earth!

So, when will we meet again?

I am looking forward to meeting you, because, "SURPRISE," if you have read this book, it means that you already are in the **"Heart Connection!"**

And you are simply interested to know more on the subject, finding tips, as I am, in order to stay in it as long as possible!

Because the "Heart Connection" activates the Law of Attraction, we do not know which pleasures Life has in store for us! …

And, as I have written earlier:

The more we are into the "Heart Connection," the more we meet people who also are in the "Heart Connection."

So, rest assured that if I see you on the street, I will recognize you! … Especially if I see the brightness and luminous shine of the "Heart Connection" in your eyes!

"Birds of a Feather Flock Together!"

I look forward to meeting you! With lots of Love from the "Heart!" Peace and Happiness!

Marie-Josée Laguerre

 | THE MENTAL, EMOTIONAL AND PHYSICAL RELIEF

Glossary

The honorary title **"Grand Master"** can be used in different contexts:

– **"Grand Master"** is the traditional title usually given to the leader of an order or a brotherhood. They are the ones who have received an initiation and have been informed a secret of the wisdom of the great. (Definition from Larousse 2000 dictionary)

– A **"Grand Master"** is a figure who receives a lot of human powers and in-depth knowledge of the spiritual realm.

– The **MASTER** shows their mastery of a discipline that they then share through their theoretical and practical education to STUDENTS who have shown a great interest for this discipline and that particular teacher.

"The **MASTER appears when the STUDENT is ready."**

The term Grand Master is still used as a unique title:

– In chess, Grand Master (GM) is the highest title a chess player can attain, it is given by the International Chess Federation.

– In the Japanese Martial Arts, the term **"Grand Master"** (Söke) is used to describe the teacher responsible for a lineage or style. The title **"Grand Master"** or **"Master"** is used to describe some senior or experienced martial artist.

Website reference: Wikipedia, The Free Encyclopedia

You will find in Chapter XI, section 2 (The Benefits of Breathing, Prana Source of Life!) information about a breathing exercise on "Inner Peace" that you can do anywhere in order to feel calm and inner peace quickly in your life.

"Make-believe": To make someone believe things that are not true, to abuse someone's credibility.
Make believe, pretend, to fool oneself.

1) "**Namaste**" or *namaskar* or *namaskaram* is commonly used to say hello and goodbye in India and is also widely used in Nepal. "Namaste" means "greetings" and "namaskar" has a more religious meaning (literally "I salute – or I bow – to your form"). The expression is often translated by "I salute the divine in you," even if that is not a literal translation.

2) According to tradition, there are three ways to do it, but always with the palms together.

A) Hands above the head, greeting God.

Greeting the Divine

B) Palms together to the forehead, greeting the spiritual guide or the Guru.

Greeting the Spiritual Guide

C) Palms together to the chest, greeting others.

Greeting our peers:
"The most popular form for the Namaste is the peer greeting"

For those who do not do yoga, I must give you some details. At the end of a class, it is common for the students and the teacher to say "Namaste" to each other.

People do it almost systematically, without really knowing what it means. When I ask other students what it means, if they do not know, I tell them that it means "THANK YOU" in Sanskrit.

"Thank you" is powerful, but "Namaste" covers more ground, "it recognizes the other as ourselves."

Namaste is "Thank You" in Sanskrit

Definition of Namaste: My soul greets yours. In you, I greet this space where the entire Universe resides. In you, I greet light, love, beauty, peace because these things are also in me. Because we share all these qualities, we are bound, we are alike, we are one.

It is exciting, isn't it? From now on, I know that you will not look at the other students and the yoga teacher the same when you say,

"Namaste." You might feel a shiver of joy deep within your heart. Namaste!

Website Reference: Wikipedia, The Free Encyclopedia

3) **Namaste: Mudra Anjali**

The Mudra Anjali (Namaste) is commonly used in Yoga and Tao techniques. It is what we call prayer hands. This Mundra balances the whole body and improves the immune system. It centers the mind and calms the anxiety. It is a symbol of honor and benediction that we also call "NAMASTE." The right hand represents the Sun, the left hand, the Moon. By joining them together, you allow a connection between the spiritual and the material world. Join your hands in front of your chest, on the heart chakra, to fully feel love and peace.

The Atmanjali – Namaste

**The Atmanjali, the prayer mudra, the
mudra of request, but also of gratitude.**

Website reference: omalayatravel.com

Aeracura" is the "Goddess of Prosperity for monetary emergencies." Celtic Goddess corresponding to Proserpine, associated with the god of the Underworld Sucellus as well as with Dis Pater, in Aquilea.

Goddess Aeracura

We know her because her statue was found in Switzerland and magical markings were found in Austria, on which she is sometimes associated with Cerberus and sometimes to Ogmios.

The statue that bore her name, "**Aeracura**," appears as a woman carrying a basket full of apples on her knees, which reminds one of prosperity and abundance. This representation is similar to the one of the German Goddess Nehalennia, even if they have very different geographical origins. "Aeracura" is known to be a Goddess of the Earth and the Underworld and was worshipped (according to markings found) in numerous sites scattered in Europe. "Aeracura" in Roman mythology is among the Novensides divinities.

God/Divine Guidance 61-63

The notion of "**God**" or "**Divine Guidance**" refers to the absolute power of the Source of Life. Some call it the power of the Universe, Source of Life, Supreme Greatness, Krishna, Yahweh, Elohim, Allan, God, Jehovah, Jesus or Buddha. In the traditional conception of the main religions, "**God**" is seen as the "**creator and source of all that exists.**"

He is attributed perfection, infinitude, immutability, eternity, goodness, omniscience, omnipotence and omnipresence.

The notion of "**God**" is directly linked to the "**Almighty Divine**" that shines with the depth of its love and infinite abundance, and it manifest itself in our lives by graces and all kinds of blessings. We can give it the name that we want and that we feel good about, as long as it is a synonym of "**Supreme Greatness.**"

French Website reference: Onelittleangel.com

Ignorance 75

The fact of not knowing something, of not being aware of something, of ignoring something.

Lack of knowledge or lack of experience in a given field.

Example: The person admits their ignorance on this subject.

General lack of education, of intellectual knowledge. Lack of knowledge, of general knowledge.

<u>Thoughts-Forms</u> 92-112-125-136

The Ancients recognize the idea that every human unconsciously generates psychological energies that are called "**Thought-Forms**". The esoteric schools of the 19th century gave the name "Thought-Forms" to these energies produced by the psyche.

▶ A Thought-Form is the realization of a thought that we communicate or relay in a spatiotemporal location specific to our "personality."

▶ The Thought-Forms (TF) are automatically created by our limbic system or emotional brain.

The more we nourish a TF, the more it attracts events that will reinforce it. A TF is a force that activates as soon as it is created.

▶ A Thought-Form (TF) is an experienced emotion that remains in memory, a belief about oneself. The Thought-Form entity is always of our creation, but it is not US.

▶ A Thought-Form is created following an emotion, something stressful or a psychological choc. The energy released at that moment will be conveyed by the person's mind who is expressing it and will finally materialize in the astral world. The power of our thoughts is immense and holds an unsuspected power.

▶ In fact, the TF will most likely materialize in the mental aura of the person who is expressing it. The TF is always created in the mental plane, which explains why a form of life who has not developed, or has not developed enough, its mind and the concepts coming with it will not be bothered by Thought-Forms.

▶ A TF is always negative, because it is created with stagnant and painful thoughts, and traumas that need fixing.

The emotions that allow the Thought-Forms of the ego to exist do something very concrete in the process because a big part of the TF stem from the third chakra (solar plexus) that is directly linked to the emotional plane.

▶ **The fourth chakra (the Heart) is never at the root of a TF because it cannot generate any negative energy, only positive.**

▶ In the case of an illness, the role of a Thought-Form is to make us remember something that we did not understand or process… **Behind an illness, there is always a Thought-Form.**

It is always the TF closer to the physical body that triggers an illness. An illness of the physical body always comes from a TF that originates from a memory. This memory can stem from this current life or from a past life.

▶ When a TF comes into action, it quickly stimulates an emotion. Our immune system protects us, but will become deficient under the weight of emotions.

A Thought-Form will be reactivated by:

– a word;

– an action;

– a situation.

Without Thought-Forms, there is no:

– sickness;

– accidents;

– unsettling difficulties in relationships or with family.

▶ A TF is not our enemy, it is only there to remind us of our history. A TF does not lie, we can only transform it, change it into something else after we have worked on Ourselves.

▶ A TF can also be collective if it belongs to a family, peoples, a group of people on a large scale, in that case, it is called an egregore.

Jean-Paul Thouny – Energy therapist, Voiron (Isère) France @2013
French Website reference: energie-sante.net and lescheminsde lenergie.com.

"Karma," or *karman* in Sanskrit, means **"act"** or **"action,"** which is action in all its forms.

In a more religious sense, it refers to ritualistic action. It is also a notion that commonly means the cycle of the causes and consequences linked to existence of sensible beings. It is the sum of what someone has done, is doing, and will do.

It is a fundamental principle acknowledged by three major Indian religions and is based on the conception of human life as a link in a chain of lives (samsara), each life being determined by the actions of the person in the previous one.

The "karma" is the reflection of our past actions that manifests in our present life.

Principle of Hinduism that means that the life of humans depends on their past actions and past lives.

Example: I don't know what I did in my previous lives to deserve my current life… Some Karma!

Website reference: Wikipedia, The Free Encyclopedia

"Chakra" from Sanskrit means "wheel" or "disc," its phonetic pronunciation is "tchakra" in English.

This term is now known to designate the "spiritual centers" or junction points of energy channels that come from a conception of Kundalini yoga and that could be located in the human body. According to this concept, there are seven main "chakras" and thousands of secondary **"chakras."**

– The seven main **"chakras"** are described as a luminous crown (silver crown) starting at the base of the spine all the way to the base of the head.

– Each **chakra** is associated to a specific color, a pair of divinities, a classical element, a variety of actions and senses, functions of consciousness, sounds, etc.

Chart of the 7 Chakras :
Colors, Sounds, Elements and Locations

COLOR	CHAKRA	LOCATION	ELEMENT	ASSOCIATED DEITY	SOUND	NUMBER OF PETALS
VIOLET	7-SAHASRARA	FONTANELLE/ CROWN OF THE HEAD	VIBRATION	SHRI PARAMASHIVA		A THOUSAND
DARK BLUE INDIGO	6-AJNA	THIRD EYE/ OPTIC CHIASM	SPIRIT	SHRI MAHAGANESHA	OM	TWO
LIGHT BLUE CYAN	5-VISHUDDHA	THROAT	ETHER	SHRI KRISHNA	HAM	SIXTEEN
GREEN AND PINK	4-ANAHATA	HEART	AIR	SHRI DURGA	YAM	TWELVE
YELLOW	3-MANIPURA	NAVEL	FIRE	SHRI VISHNU	RAM	TEN
ORANGE	2-SVADHISTHANA	SACRUM/HARA	WATER	SHRI BRAHMA	VAM	SIX
RED	1-MULADHARA	PERINEUM	EARTH	SHRI GANESHA	LAM	FOUR

THE 7 CHAKRAS: FUNCTIONS OF CONSCIOUSNESS

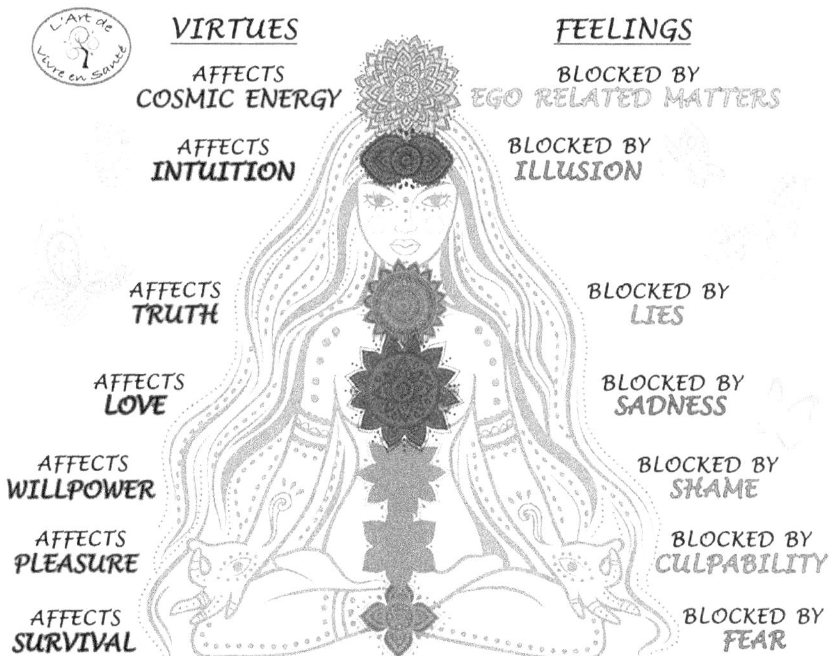

The "**Chakras**" have the ability to regulate the "energy" between different parts of the body and between the body, the Earth and the Universe. Subject to the person's health risks, they show signs of rigidity or of slowing down, of burden or of loss of vitality. They communicate among themselves and are able to balance each other out. In the same pattern, doing something to help the "energetic harmonization" (such as acupuncture, even if acupuncture does not work directly on the chakras) would have repercussions on the person's health.

In **Chinese medicine**: Each "**chakra**" corresponds to a precise point on each meridian and interacts with their associated internal organs.

▶ **The first Chakra** is the **Muladhara**, the "**Root Chakra**" is located between the anus and the scrotum. It is related to the metabolism, the lymphatic system and the bladder. It is also related to the adrenal gland.

▶ **The second chakra** is the **Hara**, the "**Center of Energy**." It is related to the kidneys, the reproducing organs, the intestines and the immune system. Most important point of the lower burner, it controls the ovaries and testicles (the gonads).

▶ **The third chakra**, is the **Manipura**, the "**Solar Plexus**." It is related to the pancreas, the liver, the gallbladder and the digestive system (stomach). It is the most important point of the middle burner.

▶ **The fourth chakra** is the **Anahata**, the "**Heart Chakra**." It is related to the Heart, the circulatory system, the lungs and the thymus. The relation with the thymus is important with children because this gland atrophies quickly with age and has for function to produce lymphocytes at the beginning of our life. It is the most important point of the upper burner.

▶ **The fifth chakra** is the **Vishuddha**, the "**Throat Chakra**." It is the center of the respiratory system and is linked with the functioning of the thyroid gland. It is important for the neck, the voice and the hands.

▶ **The sixth chakra** is the **Ajna**, the "**Third eye.**" It is located in the governing vessel. The Governing vessel or Du Mai is the carrier of 28 acupuncture points. Its principal trajectory begins at the perineum (just before the anus), goes up the spine to the head and stops inside the top lip. It is directly related to the hypophysis and sustains the eyes and the nervous system, it is intuition's home.

▶ **The seventh chakra** is the **Sahasrara**, the "**Coronal or Sky Chakra.**" It is related to the pineal gland (epiphysis). It affects the cerebral cortex activity and the energy circulating in the body, intellectual activities, concentration and memory. It balances out the yang energy in the body. Opening the sahasrara chakra, which means "thousand petals chakra," corresponds to the accomplishment of the kundalini and is equivalent to a spiritual awakening.

Website reference: Wikipedia, The Free Encyclopedia

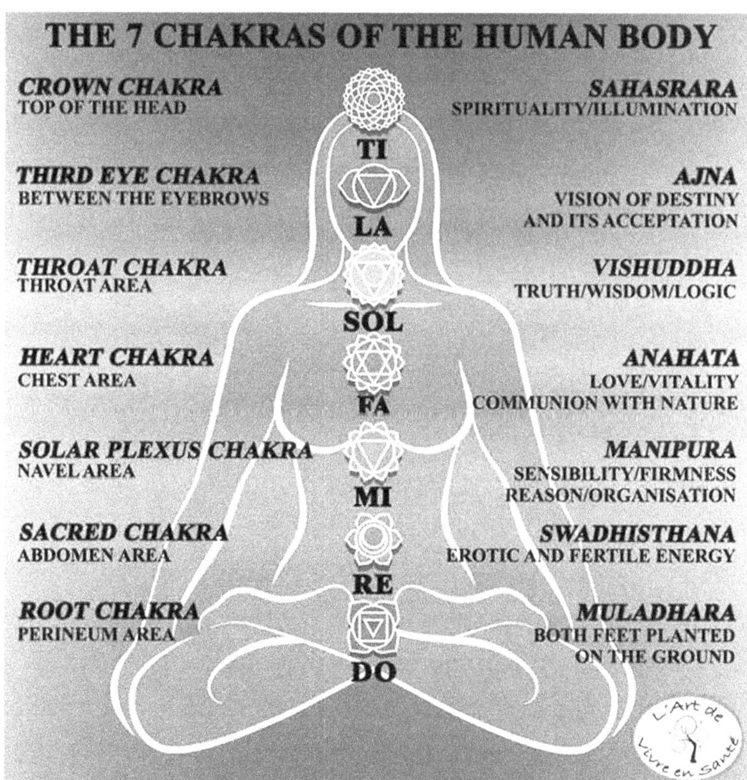

Dr. Hervé Robert has listed many health benefits in his remarkable book *Ionisation Santé-Vitalité: Les bienfaits des ions négatifs* [Health and Vitality Ionization: The Benefits of Negative Ions] published in 2008. These benefits are a better tonus, decreased fatigue, better mood, decreased infections and fewer impacts on our cardiovascular and respiratory functions. However, there has not been many studies done on the subject in France where, for a very long time, curative medicine has taken over preventive medicine.

The Russian biophysicist, Alexander Chizhevsky, is the first person to study the "negative ions." He conducted many experiments, the firsts were on animals. By cutting their supply of fresh air by using a dense woolen filter, he discovered that mice became lethargic after a few days, as if they had avitaminosis. He measured the electricity level in the cage and realized that no negative ions remained. He then sent a charge of negative ions and the animals felt a lot better.

He treated patients, in Russian hospitals, with ionic therapy and came to the conclusion that breathing **"negative ions"** strengthens immunity and leads not only to a state of general wellness, but also to a longer youth, since ionic air possesses a strong antioxidant effect.

According to **doctors**, the negative ion concentration in the **air has to be higher than 600 ions/cm3**. For your information, we should live with air filled with **1,500 to 2,000 negative ions/cm3**. However, the concentration of apartments and city offices is rarely above 100–200 ions/cm3. The air coming in a bedroom from a vent also loses ions, especially negative ions. Air conditioners also alter the electric state of the air by filtering it through cotton, a gauze, oil filters or other filters. They remove all the ions from the air!

A lack of ionization leads to hypoxia, decreased focus, fatigue and the weakening of the immune system. We spend up to 90% of our time indoors. We are still able to get the required amount of negative ions as to not be lazy and, to be healthy, we only have to go outside more! A walk in the woods or even in a park is an efficient solution to breathe in negative ions.

French Website reference: The Epoch Times

WHAT ARE THE PROVEN HEALTH EFFECTS OF "NEGATIVE IONS"?

Scientific studies have shown that atmospheres loaded with negative ions can relieve hay fever, asthma symptoms, ease seasonal depression, fatigue and headaches. It has also been shown that negatively loaded atmospheres improve the performance of voluntary movements, the ability to work, refine mental capacities and lower the error rate.

French Website reference: SensOriginal.com. General information on wellness.

OTHER HEALTH BENEFITS OF "NEGATIVE IONS"

▶ **Asthma, allergies and other respiratory problems**: Many scientific studies were done over the last couple of years (mainly in Europe and in Russia) to show how the exposition to a high level of negative ions reduces drastically and significantly asthma and allergies as well as symptoms and respiratory diseases caused by pollution.

▶ **Migraines**: Inhaling negative ions regulates the serotonin production in the brain. The overproduction of serotonin in the brain causes migraines.

▶ **Depression**: A study done by the University of Columbia suggested that the negative ions treatment is more effective than antidepressants such as Prozac and Zolof and there are no side effects.

▶ **Fatigue**: The overproduction of serotonin (chemical substance produced in the brain) can also cause fatigue. Negative ions regulate the serotonin production in the brain.

► **Sleep**: A study made in France has shown that negative ionizers help people to sleep better by regulating the serotonin production in the brain.

► **Mental performance and concentration**: Many tests have shown that people who have been exposed to negative ions have way better results in mental reflection activities than those who do not.

► **Sports performance**: Because of the test results conducted by Russian researchers on negative ionization, ionizers are always installed in Russian locker rooms and rest areas for athletes.

► **"Serious burn victims"**: Studies conducted in a hospital showed that serious burn victims who were put in that atmosphere had a better chance to recover quickly and completely.

French Website reference: SensOriginal.com. General information on wellness.

Energetic Bodies143

See also the Glossary definition for *"**Subtle Bodies**".

What is an Energetic body?

It is a general term often used in its plural form for energetic therapy and refers, for the human aura, to one of the different vibratory structures that we can differentiate on humans, they each have their own precise role.

Other expressions are used to refer to the "Energetic body": **Astral body, Mental body, Causal body, Subtle bodies, Auric fields, Eco-field, body of Light or Etheric body…**

French Website reference: Aura-couleurs.fr

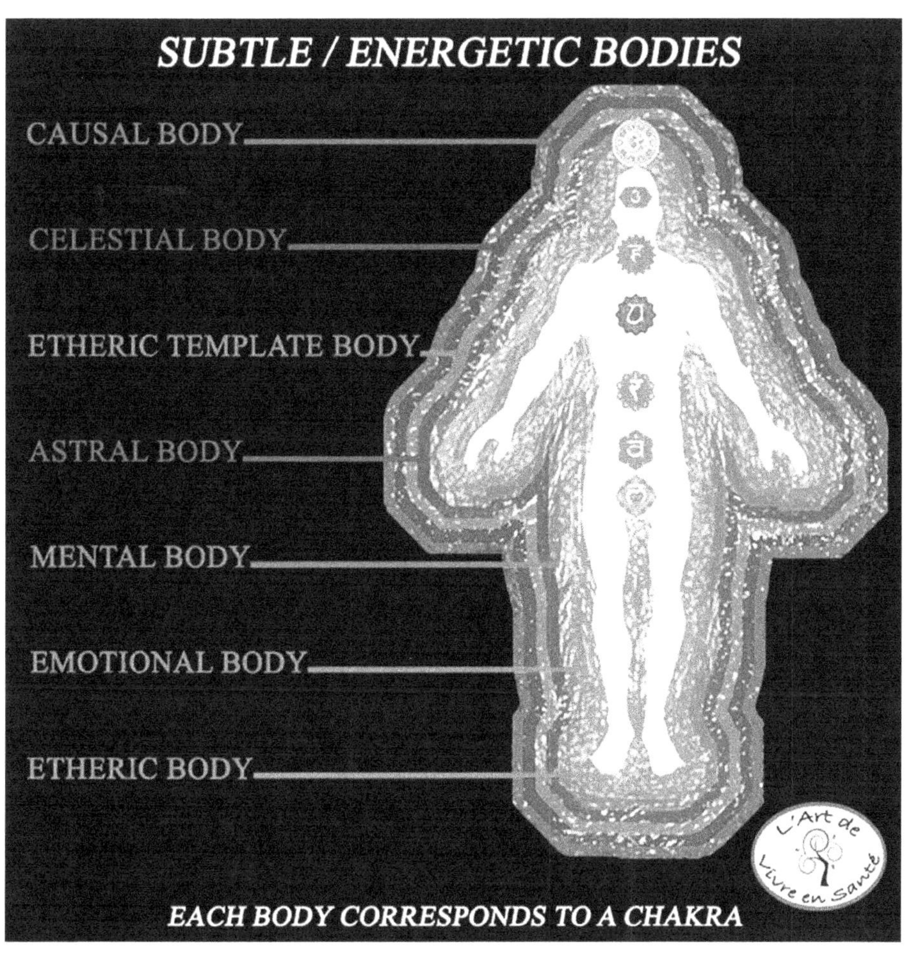

Auric Body 143

See the "Aura" definition.

Emotional Body 143

The "emotional body" is our second energetic layer and is associated to the feelings and the emotions that we feel.

The "emotional body" is what connects the physical body, the mental body and the spiritual body. The emotional body integrates all the emotions that belong to you in this life as well as emotional shocks that have not been cleaned from multiple previous lives. **You come into this world with a heavy burden**. This burden now has to be completely annihilated. It holds the key to our evolution.

The "emotional body" has many names, it is also called body of desires, body of sensibility or kamasic body (Sanskrit term for desire).

It represents a complete unit by itself and differentiate itself from the physical and mental bodies. It has its own existence, attributes and rhythms. The **"emotional body"** is an aggregate of forces that enter the conscience as desires, impulsions, strong desires, hopes, determinations, motives and projections. The **"emotional body"** allows us to connect with the sixth plane, the emotional plane, that is made of:
– emotions
– affection
– desires
– imagination

Studying the emotional body of humans will be easier if we consider its different ordinary expressions because it is by observing the effects and trying to master them that humans can become self-aware and then become a Master.

Here are the most common manifestations of astral activity:

I. Fear

II. Depression, or its opposite, euphoria

III. The Desire to quench the physical appetites

IV. The Desire for happiness

V. The Desire for liberation, aspiration

Website reference: https://sites.google.com/view/psycho-astrologie initiatique/glossaire/corps-émotionnel

Aura 146-148

1) The "Aura" is an esoteric concept referring to a colored outline, like a "halo of light" shining around the body or the head of a living

being which would be the manifestation of one or many "energy fields" or a vital energy.

2) The human "Aura" is both an energy field and the reflection of the body's vital energies.

These energies define who we are and are defined themselves by our environment and our lifestyle.

The Aura reflects our health, our nature, our mental activity and our emotional state. It also often shows illnesses way before the first symptoms.

The "Aura" is an energetic layer of different colors with an ovoid shape that surrounds the body of every living being. In humans, the Aura is comprised of many layers where the vital energy flows. Every layer interacts with the physical body through chakras.

There are seven main energetic bodies with their own energetic vibrations. They surround the physical body in successive layers, like Russian nesting dolls, and form a growing energetic field.

THE 7 BODIES

3) The first three layers represent the physical body's energy. The fourth one represents the astral body. The top three layers are the celestial body's energetic vibrations.

4) **The 7 different Aura layers:**

– **The Etheric body** (Physical): It is the exact reflection of the physical body on the subtle plane. This body is loaded with our vital energy, the one that gets denser to form matter…

– **The Emotional body**: It is our second energetic layer and is associated with the feelings and emotions that we feel.

– **The Mental body**: It is the headquarters of thought, imagination, reasoning and what is innate and acquired. It is the transition between the material plane and the mental plane.

– **The Astral body**: It acts as a "double" drain for the "earthly heaviness" and can take any form and go through every solid structure.

– **The Etheric Template body**: It bears the imprint of all the causes and effects of our life events (all our lives…). Karma intervenes at this level.

– **The Celestial body** (Buddhist): It is the awareness of being unified, connected with every existing thing. When we reach that point of existence, we feel as if we were connected to the entire Universe. We see the light and the love in every existing thing.

– **The Causal body**: It is where we get the awareness that we are ONE with ALL and ALL in ONE…

5) **Aura and vitality**: The Aura's composition varies from one person to the next. A healthy person has a more developed Aura than someone at the end of their life.

When the Aura is weakened, it is unable to maintain its energy. It is possible to strengthen an Aura through positive thinking, meditation, chromotherapy, etc.

THE 7 LAYERS OF THE AURIC FIELD

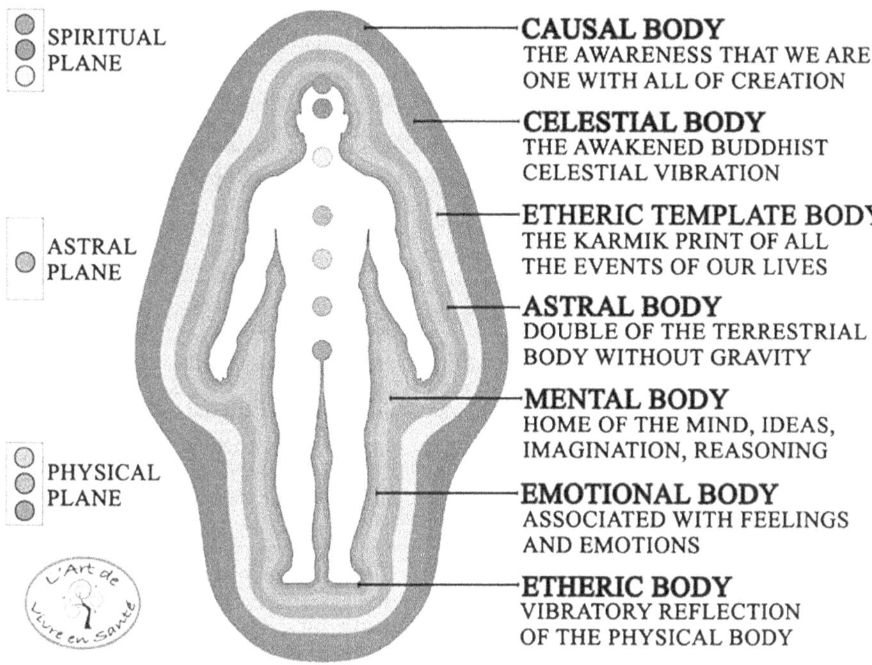

6) **The colors of the Aura**: The colors of the Aura are not constant, they vary according to our health, our mood and our spiritual elevation. Do not be surprised by the changes in your color preferences, whether it be for interior decoration or how you dress. The mind and the Aura are closely connected.

Remember that even if there are multiple colors for an Aura that blend, there is still a dominant color.

AURA COLORS AND THEIR MEANING

RED	**Bright:** Energy, vitality, determination, willpower, dynamism, positivity, generosity, material health **Dark:** Fear, anger, mischief, hate, pride, rigidity, selfishness, arrogance, love of power
ORANGE	**Bright:** Courage, joy of living, artistic creativity, sympathy, spontaneity, intellectual rapidity, audacity, confidence **Dark:** Distrust, instability, laziness, egocentricity, concern, impulsivity, extravagance, melancholy
YELLOW	**Bright:** Elevation of the intellect, creative intelligence, optimism, sincerity, clear mind, flexibility of adaptation, resilience **Dark:** Cunning, greed, selfishness, twisted mind, intellectual pride, nervousness, lack of character
GREEN	**Bright:** Color of the Heart, unconditional love, goodness, balance, healing, harmony, flexibility, logic, perseverance, justice **Dark:** Deception, jealousy, prejudice, narrowmindedness, resentment, lack of sympathy, materialism
CYAN BLUE TURQUOISE	**Bright:** Intuition, inspiration, fate, patience, comprehension, communication skills **Dark:** Perversion, indifference, coldness, pity, hypersensitivity, negative spirituality
BLUE INDIGO	**Bright:** Compassion, calm, serenity, dignity, strength, rigor, discipline, perseverance, organisation, attention to detail, search for authentic truths, devotion, wisdom, tranquility, perspicacity, telepathy **Dark:** Fear of the future, fear to face the truth, fear to tell the truth, pessimism, pride, intellectualisation
VIOLET	Spiritual ideals, spiritual evolution, altruism, purity, peace
PINK	Sophistication, modesty, friendship, devotion, loneliness, will to live, spontaneity, emotional state, tenderness, affection
BLACK	Spite, hate, conflict, destruction, dark side, immoral thoughts, bad actions, violence
WHITE	Very rare; spiritual perfection, reaching enlightenment, Christ Consciousness
GOLDEN	High spirituality, full consciousness, Divine perfection, canalisation, very high intuition

– **Red:** In the Etheric aura, red has the lowest visible vibration. It has a double nature: in its positive form, when it is clear and shiny, it represents energy, warmth and vitality.

In its negative form, it has belligerent spirit looking for rebellion and represents anger, mischief, hate and a destructive spirit. When it is very dark, the red stands for selfishness and a lack of dignity. A deep red usually stands for passion. When it turns brownish, the passion becomes unhealthy and harmful. A brown colored red indicates fear, and when the brown darkens and turns black, it indicates malice. When it has a glint of yellow, the red shows desire and controlled emotions. A pale red indicates a nervous temper, and when it is shinier and lighter, it indicates vitality, generosity and material health. Pink hints show a filial affection and love for our home while pinkish-red means happiness and tenderness.

– **Orange**: In its lighter shade, orange indicates energy and vitality. When it is redder, it appears to show egocentricity.

– **Yellow**: Yellow is the intellect color. It indicates a mundane intellect when it is dull. A brighter shade, close to gold, shows an elevated intellect purified by the mind. A dirty and muddy yellow indicates ruse, avidity and selfishness.

– **Green**: Green is for balance, the color of the Heart. Emerald green, light and shiny, is the color of healing. A large layer of emerald green in someone's aura means that the person has an interest or is involved in the art of healing. Green is the central color of the light spectrum, halfway between the poles: red and purple. Its presence in the aura also indicates balance, harmony and flexibility. In its light shade, it means harmony, peace as well as an affinity with nature and the outdoors. In its negative form, it shows a deep selfishness. When it is dirty and muddy, it shows deceitfulness and avidity. When it turns brownish, it shows jealousy.

– **Blue**: The blue color has always been associated with religious feelings and intuitive comprehension. It is also associated with healing and the Heart, just like green in its most elevated form. Blue is connected to the third eye, inspiration and a superior level of intellect. It is one of the first colors seen by the spiritual healer. When it is darker and turns indigo, it indicates a devout character and a deeply religious spirit. In its negative form, blended with brown or black, it shows a perversion of religious feelings, a fascination for the dark side of spirituality.

– **Indigo**: This color indicates a high spirituality and a diligent search for authentic truths. It can be a sign of change. It is the color of compassion, calm and serenity.

– **Violet**: Violet, a mix of red and blue, indicates a power and spiritual beliefs even more heightened. Those who have violet in their aura are the most advanced in their spiritual evolution. It is the color of royalty and it indicates a dignity of character. Violet in the aura act as an isolation and purification agent. It is not very common. It comes from superior realms and we often see it only in spiritual Masters and their followers.

When it blends in more of a lavender purple, it denotes high spirituality as well as good vitality. When it is more toward a lilac color, it expresses an altruistic and compassionate character. Violet first appears above the head in an ovoid shape that surrounds the crown chakra. As the follower evolves, it radiates from there, filling the entire aura with its light.

– **Pink**: This color is associated with refinement, modesty and deliberately chosen solitude. It is the color of the emotional body, of devotion-like attitudes, of friendship and physical love. It acts on the nervous system and revitalizes the etheric body through the emotional body. It increases the will to live.

– **Black**: Black indicates maliciousness and hatefulness. It is associated with misconduct, dividedness and dark thoughts. It is the worst color in an aura.

– **White**: White is the synthesis of every color. It indicates a complete integration and the capacity to unite. It is the color of the Christ consciousness, the color of the "I AM." It is the color of spiritual perfection, and you can only find it in people who have accomplished the union and attained illumination.

Website reference: Wikipedia, The Free Encyclopedia

7) **The Aura's range of action**: Sympathy toward another person comes from the fact that the color of your aura and theirs are in harmony. With love, when we speak of love at first sight, it is a phenomenon of auric vibrations. The dislike or the aversion to a person is due to too big a difference in the vibration and the color of the aura.

Subtle Bodies

*See also the *"Etheric body" definition.*

Western esotericism and certain Eastern religious traditions speak of the existence of **"subtle bodies"** or **"psychic bodies,"** **"suprasensible envelopes"** that cannot be perceived by the human sensory organs. Some people with extrasensory abilities say that they "see" these subtle bodies and can decode the information they contain.

There are a certain number of **"subtle bodies"**: etheric body, astral body, causal body, concentric layers, etc.

Some subtle bodies would also be the seat of "subtle centers" such as the chakras, the Hara center, the Kundalini, and would be penetrated by currents of "energy" corresponding to their nature, such as the nadis of yoga or the meridians in acupuncture. Traditional Chinese medicine, and particularly acupuncture, is based on the hypothesis of their existence.

The parapsychologist Rupert Sheldrake suggests the existence of morphic or morphogenic fields that are closer to the definition of subtle bodies.

Website reference: Wikipedia, The Free Encyclopedia

SUBTLE BODIES

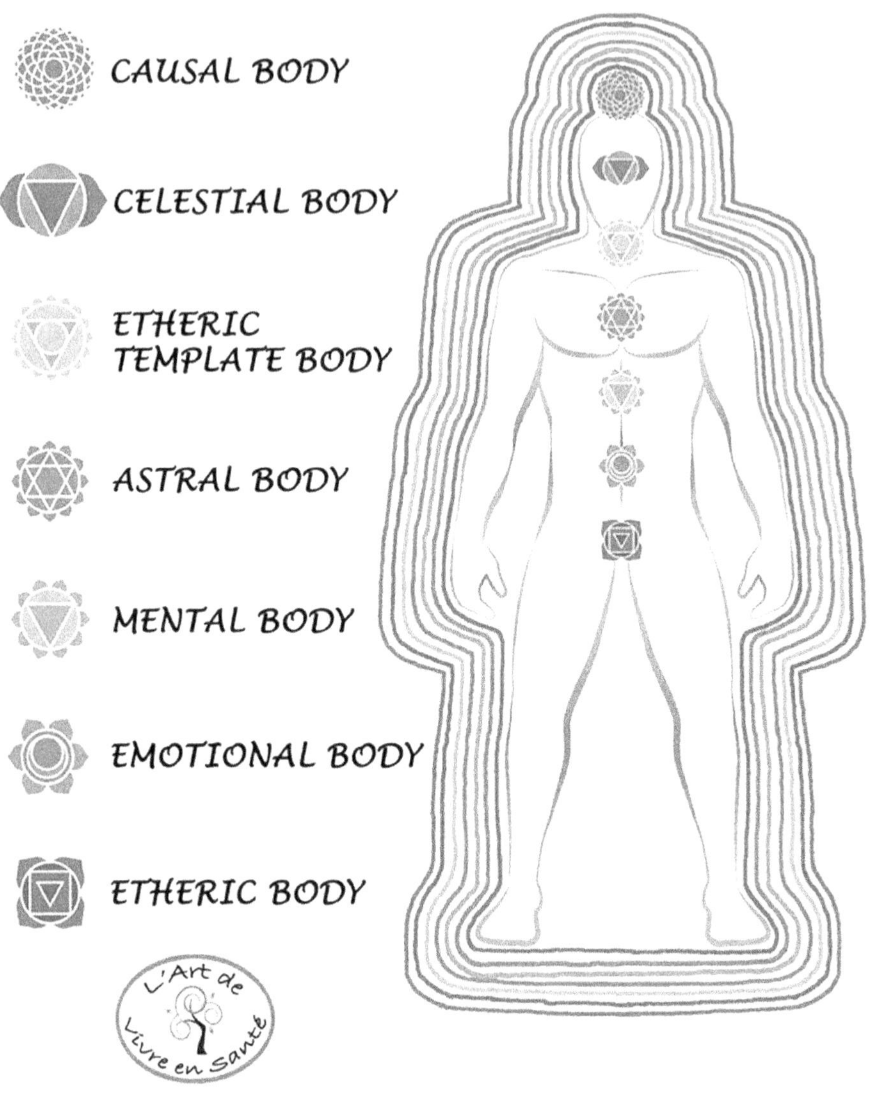

– The mental body is the seat of thought, imagination, reasoning, and what is innate and acquired. It is the transition between the material plane and the mental planes.

– The mental body is one of the subtle bodies mentioned by certain Western esoteric schools of thoughts, it is above the physical body, the etheric body and the astral body, but below the causal body.

– The mental body is the third of the seven subtle bodies.

Manifestations?

What phenomena or what experiences could confirm the existence of a "**mental body**" that is distinct from the brain and the mind?

▶ **The thought-forms**. Some thoughts have an autonomous existence, for instance fixed ideas, obsessions and mentalities. The mental body feeds the intelligence needed for concrete ideas and **dream images**. According to theosophists (Helena Blavatsky, Charles Leadbeater) and anthroposophists (Rudolf Steiner), dream images come from the mental body.

▶ **The possession**

▶ **Mental illnesses**. According to Valéry Sanfo, "many psychic disorders are a result of a bad use of the mental body. Neurosis presents an imbalance between the astral body and the mental body."

▶ **The brain and the spinal cord** are the home of the mental body, the state of their health indicates the state of the mental body.

Spiritual Body..148

The **spiritual body** is the consciousness of being unified with everything that exists. When we are at that point in existence, we feel that we are connected to the whole Universe. We see the light and the love in everything that exists.

Endorphins..156

▶ **Endorphins** are the natural hormones produced by our brain when it feels joy. These endorphins give you a feeling of happiness, satisfaction and wellness.

It is the sensation of relaxation that you feel after a nice meal, a good physical training, a good laugh or a shared intense sexual moment.

▶ **Endorphins** are produced by the **hypophysis** and the **hypothalamus** and release an opioid-like secretion, the effects of which are said to be similar to the effects felt with opium, which masks pain with a natural analgesic and transmits to your body that everything is all right. Acupuncture can release these compounds and relieve pain, at least in the short term, and leave you with a wonderful feeling of wellness.

▶ Sports, extreme happiness, great food and orgasms release **natural endorphins**, they are the ones that make you feel happy and satisfied with life.

Website reference: Le Journal des Femmes, Santé/Médecine.net

BENEFITS OF ENDORPHINS

– Less pain (analgesia)
– Slower breathing pattern
– Response to stress (well-being)
– Decreases appetite
– Helps with thermoregulation (regulation of body temperature)
– Stimulates the production of dopamine which is involved in the reward phenomenon and in certain sensations of pleasure
– Acts as an antidepressant
– Changes mood

FACTORS AFFECTING THE PRODUCTION OF ENDORPHINS

Factors increasing their production
– Pain
– Stress
– Sport (30 minutes/day multiplies by 5 the production of endorphins)
– Making love (multiplies by 5 the production of endorphins)

– Satisfaction

– Massages

– Acupuncture

– Psychotherapy

Factors decreasing their production

– Immobilization

– Malnutrition

– Chronic pain caused by exhaustion (fibromyalgia)

– Depression

EUPHORIC EFFECT OF ENDORPHIN

Many athletes say that endorphins are a natural drug. What allows you to feel the most endorphins is sport. Some athletes are therefore true addicts.

The one big advantage of endorphins is that there are no negative side effects other than the fact that you might annoy the people around you by always being in such a good mood!

French Website reference: Espace-Musculation.com

WHAT ARE THE EFFECTS OF THE RELEASE OF ENDORPHINS?

Endorphins have unsuspected effects on the human body:

– A state of euphoria

– A natural relaxant

– A powerful painkiller

– Helps with fatigue

HERE ARE SEVEN WAYS TO STIMULATE THE PRODUCTION OF ENDORPHINS:

– The smell of vanilla or lavender

– Dark chocolate

– Hot and spicy food

– Sex

– Laughter

– Sport

– Foods high in vitamin C

<u>Serotonin</u> 156

1) **Serotonin** is a central nervous system chemical messenger, a neurotransmitter, involved in several physiological functions such as sleep.

It is responsible for digestive stability, your mood, your eating habits, and sexual behaviors, as well as depression. A 2019 study found that people with depression often had low levels of serotonin. Serotonin deficiency has also been associated with anxiety and insomnia.

2) **Serotonin** impacts every part of your body, from your emotions to your motor functions. Serotonin is not only used by the brain, every main organ in the body (the heart, kidneys, lungs and liver) use it.

3) **Serotonin and mood**. Serotonin is a mood stabilizer. It is the chemical that helps you sleep, eat and digest. Low doses of serotonin have been associated with depression.

4) **Serotonin also helps with:**
– Regulating anxiety, happiness and your mood
– Reducing depression
– Healing wounds
– Helping to control nausea
– Maintaining great bone health

Serotonin helps you to naturally regulate your mood. Here is how you will feel when your levels of serotonin are normal:
– happier
– calmer

– more focused

– less anxious

– more emotionally stable

5) **Serotonin and physical activity**: regularly practicing physical activity helps boost the natural production of serotonin.

Website reference: Wikipedia, The Free Encyclopedia

<u>Sauna, Comparing the Different Types of Saunas</u>.155

We can choose between different types of saunas according to the energy that is used.

There is the traditional sauna with either a wood or a gas heater, the sauna with an electric heater and the infrared sauna.

Traditional Sauna, outside view

Traditional sauna with wood burning heater

Traditional sauna with wood burning heater

Sauna with an electric heater/Sprinkling of water over the rocks

Sauna with an electric heater/Sprinkling of water over the rocks

Infrared Sauna, inside view

Infrared Sauna, outside view

Bibliography

Weekend Yoga/Tao activities 134
Marie-Josée Laquerre.com 450 712-7928 – Canada
Website: L'Art de Vivre en Santé.com

Songs 137
Feu, feu, joli feu… *Les litanies du feu*
French folk music, 1940, Carnet de chants Cocorico!
Lyrics by Léon-Robert Brice. To the tune of *Vin gaulois*, well known
to the Scouts de France.

Fasting 139
Magazine Nature, 2016

The ten benefits of lemon water 140-141
Dr. Alain Tuan Qui, French Website reference: Docteur Bonne
Bouffe.com.

Lagacé Jacqueline, Ph. D. (2011). *Comment j'ai vaincu la douleur et l'inflammation chronique par l'alimentation*, Éditions Fides.

2,600,000 sold all around the world! … in 23 languages.
Bourbeau, Lise. (Septembre 2000), Les Éditions E.T.C. Inc.
Rejection, abandonment, humiliation, betrayal and injustice: five fundamental wounds at the origin of our physical, emotional and mental suffering.

Lise BOURBEAU, author of 27 best-sellers sold worldwide in more than 8 million copies, is the founder of E.T.C. Éditions Inc – Écoute Ton Corps. The School "Listen To Your Body – International" is the largest school of personal development in Québec. Her books (27), all best-sellers, have been translated into several languages (26): French, English, Chinese, Korean, Spanish, German, Italian, Russian, Portuguese, Japanese, Greek, Croatian, Lithuanian, Romanian, Polish, Bulgarian, Estonian, Swedish, Slovakian, Dutch, Czech, Turkish, Hungarian and others, and are distributed in 34 European countries and in Canada.

Author of 17 books, Director of "L'École international des Rêves," founded in 1992, and international Conference Speaker.
Website reference: Art de Rêver.

About the Author

Focused on her desire to contribute to the wellness and the quality of life of people on a daily basis, Marie-Josée Laquerre has been interested by the wellness field for the last 25 years.

Having 18 years of experience as the owner of a **Wellness Center/Spa (Balneotherapy, Massotherapy and Wellness treatments)**, Marie-Josée now follows her passion of sharing her "**Health Favorites**" in her blogs, on her social networks and her website **lartdevivreensante.com**. Her objective is to share all her best knowledge and therapeutic products that have had an impact in her own life.

As a **Certified TTC International Yoga Teacher**, she teaches on the weekend for Yoga/Tao Retreats. It is in Guadeloupe, in 1996, that she teaches her first Tao workshop (vital energy stimulation techniques) and opens her first Wellness Center/Spa of Balneotherapy and Massage Therapy.

Passionate about the science of numbers, she completed her training to become a **Professional Numerologist** at the Université Laval in Québec.

Since then, she continues to practice in private consultations and is an authority in the field. She did her university studies in **Communications and Psychology** at that same university.

In addition, she has taken a full 3-year training in **personal development and metaphysics** (helping relation and causes of unease and illnesses). It provided her the necessary ease and expertise for her counselling in helping relations.

For many years, she shared her knowledge on many subjects, on wellness and health, through written media like journals and health magazines. You can also hear her on the radio section of the website: **lartdevivreensante.com** on the radio show "**Les Coups de Cœur de Marie-Jo**".

As a "Health Investigator," she has always been curious to discover and learn the most effective ways to take care of oneself. It then became a "**Life Mission**" to experiment and share them. She makes it her duty to test and communicate the experiences she acquired over the years on the "Art of healthy living." Her intention is to contribute to people's quality of life, motivated by the gift of self and dedication to others. Her human kindness and benevolence were rewarded by the **Governor General of Canada**, Mrs. Adrienne Clarkson, who awarded her an **Honourable Mention for Act of Bravery** after she saved a man from drowning. Following this significant event, creating her daily life with joy and love became her priority, which she affectionately calls her little "**SME of Happiness!**"

Overcoming a difficult trial and bouncing back in the face of adversity has led to a beneficial transformation in her life. A lesson that has shown her that "Love conquers all."

According to the author, the best guide to "Happiness in Everyday Life" is right there, within Us!

As she says:

"Choosing your 'HEART' is choosing to BE HAPPY!"

Acknowledgements

Since the beginning of the writing process of this book, **"The Heart Connection,"** I feel personally inclined to be grateful for the realization of this project and I feel a lot of gratitude for this great gift from Life. It is with a lot of enthusiasm that I say, **"Merci la Vie !"** … which, strangely enough, was the first title of this book!

Even if I have found this process long and exhaustive, I have loved every step to create a manuscript. I have learned a lot in a field with which I was not acquainted at all, forcing me to go out of my comfort zone.

This book has really helped go through the uncertainties of Life, it has put a damper on a lot of sadness, wounds and loss, as well as facilitate a new and fulfilling direction for my life.

I must thank some remarkable people in my life who have been witnesses of this **"Life Transition"**.

I thank my other half, the "man of my dreams," my partner Michel, who has been an immeasurable presence. He helped me daily with everything, he continuously supported me to ensure that my determination would not falter and that I could reach my objectives.

"Thank you, my sweet love, you truly are a man of the heart!"

I would also like to sincerely thank my immediate family, my mother, Aline Laquerre, and my sister, Manon, my good friends, and good acquaintances, who have all given me unconditional support. Loving people who have been there for me and listened to me while this transition was unfolding.

Thank you from the bottom of my heart to my sister, Manon Laquerre, for the linguistic revision of the French version of this book. I felt supported all the way through this project, thanks to her encouraging presence, her availability, her developed analytical mind and her useful comments. "Thank you, my dear sister, I love you!"

And thank you, dear readers, to have taken the time to read this book, and if you feel like it, to share this book… As more "human beings" start to live in synchronicity in **The Heart Connection,** *our home, this Earth, will become a space where respect and love are ever-present!*

Marie-Josée Laquerre

Table of contents

www.ingramcontent.com/pod-product-compliance
Lightning Source LLC
LaVergne TN
LVHW050558200726
843508LV00010B/1676